Arthur Brühlmeier

Head, Heart and Hand

Education in the Spirit of Pestalozzi

Translated by Mike Mitchell

Sophia
Books

in association with

PestalozziWorld
educating children for a better life

Sophia Books

40 Devonshire Road, Cambridge, CB1 2BL, United Kingdom
Sophia Books is an imprint of Open Book Publishers CIC Ltd.

ISBN: 978-1-906924-99-7

Cover picture: An 1846 lithograph by G. Balder based on a drawing of Johann Heinrich Pestalozzi at the age of seventy two, by the Estonian artist Gustav Adolf Hippius (1788–1856)

All paper used by Sophia Books is SFI (Sustainable Forestry Initiative), and PEFC (Programme for the Endorsement of Forest Certification Schemes) Certified.

Printed in the United Kingdom and United States by Lightning Source for Sophia Books

Head, Heart and Hand

The Author

After training as a primary school teacher in Wettingen (Canton Zurich, Switzerland), Arthur Brühlmeier was for seventeen years head of a school for children aged from seven to fifteen, after which he studied Education, Psychology and Journalism at the University of Zurich, finishing with a dissertation on 'Developments in Pestalozzi's Thought.' He subsequently worked in teacher training as a lecturer in Educational Theory, Educational Practice and Psychology. He has spent the last twenty years at the teacher training college in Zug (Switzerland), where he was involved in a project on the concept of 'teacher training as personality training'; he was also able to introduce a number of reforms grounded in the spirit of Pestalozzi's ideas.

Brühlmeier has edited three editions of writings by Pestalozzi, including a two-volume edition for the People's Republic of China. He has written numerous articles on themes relating to psychology and educational theory and practice (see www.bruehlmeier.info) and is also involved in the management of the extensive Pestalozzi website (www.heinrich-pestalozzi.de).

Arthur Brühlmeier's interests outside education include music, botany and black-and-white photography, for which he has had several exhibitions. He has been married since 1961 and has five grown-up children.

Contents

Linguistic note:

The text that follows discusses teachers, pupils and politicians. Since such designations occur innumerable times, I hope the reader will understand if, in the interest of readability, I have refrained from using 'he or she', 'his or her' all the time. When I refer to teachers and pupils as 'he' it is the function of the person I have in mind, not their sex. I thank in advance all my female readers who are happy to accept this and to concentrate on my ideas in the interest of education.

A.B.

Preface to the English edition

The aim of this book is to familiarise English-speaking readers with the thoughts of the educationalist and philosopher, Johann Heinrich Pestalozzi (1746–1827) and at the same time to show that consideration of these fundamental ideas can provide helpful guidance for all those who want schools to be more child-oriented and produce better-educated school leavers. My practice as a teacher on all levels of the nine years of compulsory education in Switzerland and as a lecturer in Education and Psychology at different teacher training establishments has confirmed my belief that Pestalozzi had an uncommonly clear vision of the essential laws behind teaching and learning and that his insights are by no means restricted to his own time, but are timeless in their relevance. My own experience comes from decades of teaching in Switzerland and I am therefore most closely acquainted with current problems in Swiss schools and education in general, but I am convinced that the areas I deal with in the twenty-seven chapters of this book will be felt to be problematic — to a greater or lesser extent — in all modern countries and that each and every reader will be well able to relate what I say to conditions in their own land.

I would also like to bring to English readers' attention the man who was the first to make a determined effort to acquaint people in Britain with Pestalozzi's ideas, James Pierpont Greaves (1777–1842). At the age of forty he came to join Pestalozzi in Yverdon, where he worked for four years as an English teacher, at the same time doing all he could to make Pestalozzi's teaching methods more widely known. Thus he recommended Pestalozzi's methods in a detailed memorandum to the English Prime Minister in 1818 and also encouraged Pestalozzi to compose a systematic presentation of his ideas for British mothers. Pestalozzi took up his suggestion and wrote the famous thirty-four letters to Greaves, which were then translated into English by Christian Friedrich Wurm; in 1827 Greaves had them published at his own expense under the title of *Letters on early Education — addressed to J. P. Greaves, Esq. by Pestalozzi* (W. Sears, London). The German original has unfortunately been lost, so that Greaves' book has been used as the basis for a retranslation into German and for translations into other languages. The high regard in which this book is held lies in the fact that in no other work did Pestalozzi express his ideas on education so systematically and in such concrete detail. Its significance has led Google to put the original 1827 edition on the Internet.

For me the foremost of the present-day institutions that acknowledge their indebtedness to Pestalozzi and his ideas is PestalozziWorld. Inspired and directed by Sir Richard Butler, this organisation for educational aid operating mainly in Asia and Africa is indirectly responsible for my writing the German version of *Head, Heart and Hand*: one of PestalozziWorld's sponsors had come across the article 'Teaching in the Spirit of Pestalozzi', which I had written for their schools, and promised me his support for a more extensive publication. I would therefore like to express my heartfelt thanks both to PestalozziWorld, which has now made this book possible, and to the generous sponsor. Particular thanks are also due to François von Hurter, who took charge of the project, to Mike Mitchell for his professionalism and persistence in assuring both Pestalozzi's and my own thinking came across in English, and to Joanna Nair, who gave the English manuscript a critical reading.

Arthur Brühlmeier
September 2009

'Educated humanity is a blessing
for the world.'

Educating in the Spirit
1 of Pestalozzi

The importance of education for the moral, technological and economic development of society and state is well known all over the world. In many countries the education system has been subject to permanent, in part even dramatic change for years, if not decades. That would not be happening if the powers that be were generally satisfied with the educational standards. It is a fact that when they leave school, many students have not reached the required level — measured against the official curriculum — and in many areas their knowledge is often scanty.

It is also a fact that educational policies in many countries are creating increasing pressure on those involved. Schools are more tightly organised, teamwork is a requirement for teachers and they are bound by quality-assurance systems developed on scientific principles. Heads are given wider powers, hierarchical structures are strengthened. In many EU countries, and in non-EU Switzerland as well, courses at universities and other institutions of higher education are strictly organised down to the last detail according to the 'Bologna' model, which originated in America and has become the official norm in many EU countries. In this system, students have to work through a prescribed number of topics in standardised time units. What is being looked for is not education, and certainly not education at leisure, but efficient and cost-effective training — young people are to be fitted for tasks in the economy and administration. Standardised report cards, which mean the same everywhere in the world, are to record the results of standardised courses which can be recognised in other countries and qualify the graduate for a particular step on the career ladder.

Doubtless all these and any future measures have been and will be taken with the best of intentions. Despite that, I consider much of what has been done ineffective and counterproductive. The reforms are too one-sided in orientation. They seem to reflect a blindness to the problems thousands of teachers are wrestling with every day. All the political effort is focused on the reorganisation of *structures*, there is a lot of talk of money and of systems but hardly any of children, of pupils, of individual teachers and the demands made on them by educational theory and practice which they are often scarcely able to meet any more. Nor is there talk of time, of taking one's time, of thoroughness. Pupils seem to be looked on as empty vessels that can be filled at will as long as the regulations, syllabuses and textbooks have been compiled accordingly. If a new problem crops up anywhere, there is an immediate call for a new school subject. That kind of thing looks good because it proves that one wants to get to the root of the problem, but it is rare that anyone asks whether the pupils, teachers and the school as a whole can cope with it and what cuts other objectives must suffer.

This raises the question whether any of those who are behind this constant expansion of the curriculum have ever been present when parents were desperately trying to help their unmotivated and so far unsuccessful child not to get left behind. Have they any idea of the scenes there are in many homes because the children don't enjoy going to school? Because they are confused by all the things that have to be 'gone through' in class, but not thoroughly practised, and are often — together with their despairing parents — at the end of their tether. Or do they have a magic wand the teacher can wave when extremely spoilt children, as if it were a matter of course, make disparaging comments about or arrogantly reject any demand that requires them to make an effort?

But how is it that a large proportion of our fellow citizens have come to believe that changes in the system aimed at the standardisation and hierarchical management of the educational process, as well as more intensive use of technical resources, can really improve the quality of education? We have been going down that road for many years and yet one could not really say that there has been any clear improvement in educational attainment. My own assessment is that trust in the above-mentioned measures remains undiminished because those with a decisive voice in educational policy, educational administration and educational research have transferred — presumably unconsciously, as a matter of course — solutions that have proved at least partly profitable in the economic field to the areas of education and school organisation. It is assumed that greater concentration of resources, tighter organisation, stricter standardisation and more efficient structures will guarantee success. *But success in education is determined by different laws than in the economy.* If this fact is ignored, all reforms degenerate into activity for its own sake. What is needed, then, is a change of focus, away from purely organisational, legal and financial factors and onto educational aims, practical matters of teaching and real everyday problems.

This means that all those who have responsibility for our children's education must be guided by the laws that operate in this area. It means bearing in mind the *essence*, the *nature* of education, learning, teaching and even the way we bring up children in general. It is a never-ending task which falls upon all generations; if we refuse to accept it, the result will be failures, confusion and suffering. The more often we call to mind the essential nature of education, the more our teaching will achieve true *quality*.

That brings me to the central theme of this book. My concern is to bring out the *essence* of education, learning and schools. My concern is to *refine* our work as educators and to bring real *quality* to students' performance.

There is a *tension* between the reality of our present-day education, dominated as it is by a belief in progress that cannot see beyond technical/organisational matters, and the essence of education — teaching and learning. It is a tension which is often hard to bear, but anyone who does not sense it, who does not expose himself to it by trying, as far as he is able, to reconcile the two aspects, will find his work does not bear fruit. He will remain a mere cog in the machinery of social processes which lack direction and constantly create more problems than they solve.

The aim of this book, then, is *encouragement*. To encourage *teachers* to devote themselves to this search for the essence of education as they go about their everyday business. I would also like to encourage *politicians* to create the conditions that would allow the teachers to use their own initiative in carrying out their task of educating children in a way that is informed by this essence. And I would also like to encourage *parents* to support their children's teachers and the authorities in all their efforts in education, which are aimed at developing true humanity.

Anyone who occupies himself intensively with education in the widest sense cannot avoid examining the ideas of truly important philosophers of education. In this respect, a practising educationalist will have different preferences according to his own geographical or philosophical background and will consult different thinkers. As a Swiss, it is natural for me to turn to a man who is probably the best-known educational reformer in the world, Johann Heinrich Pestalozzi (1746–1827). His writings reveal deep insights into the nature and vocation of mankind and reveal the ways in which a person can reach his true goal: full humanity. It was a fundamental experience of my over forty years as a teacher at practically all levels that I was always successful when I followed Pestalozzi. Therefore in this book as well I will follow Pestalozzi in my reflections on education, on learning and teaching.

But what does it mean, to follow Pestalozzi? It is certainly not to find out how Pestalozzi and his colleagues *themselves* taught and to copy that. Many of the details of the methods that were tried out in Burgdorf and Yverdon have outlived their usefulness; there is no point in trying to revive them. But it does make sense, it is helpful, to nurture within oneself the pedagogical spirit and the view of the nature and vocation of mankind which inspired a man like Pestalozzi. Many other thinkers have come to the same conclusions. They were all imbued with the same spirit. That is why I am committed to education *in the spirit of* Pestalozzi. Anyone who is open to this will not be in thrall to a system, will not be an imitator, but someone who shapes things himself, who is creatively active. Many paths will be open to him, but he will also be aware of which ones will lead him astray and that it is not sufficient to *instruct* pupils, but that they need education in the fullest sense of the word to enable them to shape their lives in a fruitful manner.

Naturally it is important to try to do well at school, to digest information, to acquire knowledge and skills, but that is not the sum total of education. Pestalozzi has shown that there is more to it than attaining prescribed learning outcomes; it is concerned with the whole person, with their physical, mental and psychological development. Only if we, as teachers, put the specific goals in the service of a higher unity will we be approaching a truly comprehensive goal: *the education of the whole person* in the spirit of Pestalozzi.

Already I can hear an objection: 'You only see the individual, you're not looking at society. Take a good look at it — the gap between rich and poor is getting bigger and bigger. Anonymous powers behind the scenes are getting more and more influential and more and more brazen. And not only young people, the whole of society is getting more and more violent. People foment wars, preach hatred and human rights are trodden underfoot. Fundamental values are ignored and millions and millions of people are caught up between manipulation, the struggle for a living and the search for pleasure. And in the race for profit the environment goes to wrack and ruin: the air, soil and water are polluted, species are dying out every day, the lungs of the world are being ruthlessly felled and monocultures, pushed by big business, are destroying the natural basis of the lives of hundreds of millions of people. And you come along talking about the individual education of the whole person!'

At that time of radical change, that turbulent period when the old society based on privilege began to give way to democracy, Pestalozzi found himself in a comparable situation. In Switzerland, where the unstable state had rested on a constitution graciously granted by Napoleon, the fall of the Emperor left a vacuum and it was highly uncertain which way things would go. In this situation the ageing Pestalozzi took up his pen and wrote his fundamental political work: *An die Unschuld, den Ernst und den Edelmut meines Zeitalters und meines Vaterlandes* (To the Innocence, Seriousness and High-mindedness of my Age and my Country). It is a passionate appeal to all those in positions of responsibility to work for law and justice. But the core of the book is his theory of education, and he formulated his belief in the lapidary sentence, 'The beginning and end of my politics is education.' For Pestalozzi, it was clear that revolutionary changes do not help people if they are not founded on the basic convictions and moral will of individuals. And this foundation can only be created by the education of the whole person. Thus Pestalozzi's final conclusion is: 'The continent has sunk so low morally, intellectually and socially, that it can only be saved by educating people in humanity, that is by forming fully rounded human beings.'

Educating people in the spirit of Pestalozzi is an ideal. It is, of course, in the nature of *all* ideals that the reality never matches up to them completely. Ideals are signposts, landmarks from which we take our bearings. They can inspire, but they can also be disheartening. The gap between what we would like to achieve and what we can achieve is really only bearable if we keep one basic fact in mind: *no one can achieve the absolute.* Failure, inadequacy, half measures are all part of life. But there is positive educational value in pupils seeing their teacher as a human being who knows his limitations, who does his best for them and does not despair.

I happily admit that it is easy to write a book about ideals but difficult to put them into practice. I myself — like most teachers, I imagine — have known days of annoyance, failure, despondency, even despair, but every time the only way out I could see was to look to ideals I recognised as valid despite my own inadequacies.

I am presenting my reflections and recommendations in twenty-six further, self-enclosed chapters, without sticking to a rigid system, which would appear artificial. The individual chapters should be regarded as pieces of a jigsaw, parts of a picture that has been built up in the course of my years of teaching. My hope is that these pieces will similarly combine to form a living picture for those who read this book.

'The general raising of the inner powers of human nature to pure human wisdom is the general purpose of education.'

2 Quality? Quality!

The man — good looking, perhaps forty — was standing outside the department store, apparently uncertain which way to turn. That gave me the courage to speak to him. 'I'm doing a little opinion poll about schools. Are you willing to answer some questions?' He nodded and I asked, 'If you can put it in one short sentence, what would you say is the basic task of primary schools?' He thought, for quite a long time, and said, 'The school should prepare young people for life.' — 'And that means?' — 'Enabling the students to take their place in society, the economy and the state.'

I thanked him, astonished. His answer was precise. I have heard variations of this answer since on a number of occasions. And really, no one can object to it.

But is that everything? Should we be satisfied if school-leavers are able, for example, to read the newspaper, operate electronic machines, fill out their tax returns, handle money, take out insurance policies and cope with many of the other similar demands of modern society? In that sense they would be prepared for life, for you can live very well, even if you never read a book, never go to a concert or a museum, hang absolute kitsch on your walls, fritter away your free time aimlessly, cannot tell a pine tree from a beech, have forgotten everything you learnt in history lessons, never pick up a pencil to do a drawing and never think about the meaning of life either. Despite all that, one can fulfil one's duties as a citizen and earn sufficient money as a useful manual or office worker.

From Pestalozzi's point of view, school should not simply enable a young person to function in society, it should help him to develop as an independent personality with all its human potential. By doing that it helps him to achieve a true *quality of life*. *The quality of education, therefore, can be measured by the quality of life that education opens up for the pupil.*

We need, therefore, to think about the *quality of life* if we are to be clear about the *quality of education.* Philosophically we are skating on thin ice, for who could deny that each person himself determines, on the basis of his individual situation, what quality of life is. But this relativism is no use to a teacher. He needs standards for his work, even if no one can prove that they are generally binding.

The question, then, is: what is quality in education, what teaching and learning goals can lead to quality of life?

My view is this: much of what we do is simply geared to *maintaining* ourselves or our species. What we do is purely for a *purpose.* We supply ourselves with calories; we move from point A to point B; we speak in order to impart information; we build houses to protect ourselves; we construct vehicles we can drive or fly so that we can travel in comfort; but mostly this is not enough for us, simply fulfilling *purposes* quickly loses its attraction. We want our activities to have *meaning*, to give us a sense of *excitement, pleasure and fulfilment.* And we can do that, for in the first place we can raise purely functional activities to a new, 'higher' level by allowing ourselves to be guided by *ethical values.* And in the second place we can do many things, which would not seem particularly necessary from a purely functional point of view, in a particularly satisfying way by allowing our activity to be guided by *aesthetic values.*

To rise above the purely functional to the ethical and aesthetic level is the essential characteristic of human *culture.* It is in this that man's spiritual nature expresses itself. It is the human spirit alone that makes this meaningful activity possible and it is only by going beyond the purely functional by turning it into a cultural activity that people can experience true quality of life.

Thus if schools want to make quality of life possible, they cannot restrict themselves to 'preparing pupils for life', that is to passing on usable knowledge and skills that can be applied directly in their future lives as adults. Rather, their task is to concern themselves with the healthy physical, mental and psychological development of the child as a whole. And this happens when *life in the school* is treated as *real life*, is not geared to the students' *future* alone but takes their *present* situation into account — and that in a way that their physical, mental and psychological capacities can be developed as broadly and as intensively as possible. Only when this is happening can one seriously talk of quality in education. Only in this way can schools make a constructive contribution to combating the cultural impoverishment that is a necessary consequence of a purely utilitarian approach. Otherwise they will suffer from the same cultural emptiness as do many people whose work is governed by utilitarian considerations alone.

I would like to use the example of language to illustrate what I am trying to put across. There is no doubt that we have achieved much, if our pupils can order information in their minds and formulate it appropriately through language. However, anyone who has that ability is at best *trained*, but not *educated* in the full meaning of the word. Genuine education demands the cultivation of speaking and language in the sense of raising it to the higher level of the aesthetic. It starts with articulation. Of course, in the first place the correct enunciation of sounds serves the purpose of better comprehensibility, but that is not the end of it. With correct and refined articulation we enter another dimension, namely that of music, and with that a new realm of experience — for both speakers and listeners — as an expression of the human spirit. Education is always a matter of seeking out and encouraging such elements, and teachers who are concerned about education and quality take every opportunity to do so.

Cultured speaking demands not simply correct articulation, but also breathing, intonation, modulation, pacing, pauses, accentuation, emphasis — all points that are of crucial significance in music as well. This is both a science and an art. People who speak professionally — actors for example — must have mastered it. But clear speech with pure sounds that is appropriate to the content must not be reserved for professionals. It is a goal that teachers who are concerned about quality always bear in mind, knowing that in so doing they will open up new areas of experience for their pupils.

Let us take the next step, which brings us to reading. A teacher who is conscious of the importance of the aesthetic dimension as a basis for quality of life will not be satisfied with the current definition of reading as the extraction of meaning. 'Reading' is more, it is *conveying* meaning, *structuring* the text by speaking it, bringing a work of art *to life* in one's own mind. Such a teacher will never be satisfied if a pupil has merely 'extracted the meaning' from a poem or piece of prose — understood it, that is. The main task — structuring the text by speech — is still to come. This task demands a much more intensive effort from the child himself than the simple understanding and absorbing of content transmitted by a text. It is only through this creative activity that he can assimilate the text — the poem, the story, the description — mentally and emotionally. And it is only this active assimilation of a piece of writing that deserves to be called 'education'.

In reading, this superior demand appears not only in the *way* texts are handled but more especially in the *choice* of texts. Current language teaching methods tend to give the pupils a range of all possible types of text production and text use, but that in no way guarantees that the beauty and deeper meaning of a poem will be a truly enriching and fulfilling experience for them. That only comes through occupying themselves intensively with really worthwhile reading material. In the long term, only a school system informed by a culture which ignores the mediocre and devotes its time, which is too short anyway, to worthwhile material, is the sure way to arouse *a love of art and literature* in young people and equip them to enjoy some quality of life. This brings us to a goal which we must at least set the students on the road to achieving, if education is to have genuine quality: namely to get them not simply to understand the texts and perhaps also read them in the way the teacher presents them in class, but to become involved, at whatever level, in literature in the widest sense.

What has been shown here in relation to speaking and reading is correspondingly valid for the promotion of good communication skills, as well as for subjects such as writing, drawing, music, gymnastics and in general when any material is to be presented in written or graphic form. The point is always to go beyond the purely functional and to guide the student into the realm of culture, to the aesthetic level. A creative teacher, for whom connections are important, will always find ways of bringing out the aesthetic or ethical element, even when pupils are learning a foreign language, dealing with mathematical problems or tackling various kinds of topic.

In this connection let us have a quick look at Pestalozzi's basic concern: whatever content pupils are dealing with, their activity should be so arranged as to develop the 'powers and faculties' that are in every human being. Put in more modern terms, that means that content-oriented 'material' education should serve 'formal' education. Presumably people will agree that teaching which looks to the higher capabilities of mankind and makes corresponding demands in quality will foster the children's faculties in a much more consistent manner than teaching which is satisfied with the purely functional. Thus a teacher who in his comments also pays attention to careful handwriting, a clear and attractive presentation and correct language can develop in the pupils a whole series of 'faculties' which will make a higher quality of life possible in many situations, for example a sense of beauty and balance, care in approaching a task, self-criticism, conscientiousness, stamina, imagination and creativity.

Naturally educational theory also deals with 'quality of education'. It has developed a series of systems to assure quality. But that is difficult, for with the usual methods of assessing learning success, the features we are presenting as the key educational element frequently slip through the net of any system. The reason is simple: the educational outcome is very difficult or impossible to measure. If with reading, for example, the goal is simply the extraction of meaning, astute questioning can establish when the meaning of a text has been understood. But how far a pupil has been enriched by a committed oral reproduction of the text or whether the urge to immerse himself in the world of literature has been developed, or further developed, can at best be determined through direct discussion with him, but not measured. In other words, true quality of education is always something more than can be assessed by learning checks and quality assurance systems. These always focus the teaching effort on the less essential aspects and in so doing tend to devalue what is truly decisive.

Therefore it can never be left to any kind of points system to determine what 'higher quality' means in education; that is always the business of teachers who are competent to do so. Yet that is not what people want to hear today, for the modern attitude demands objectivity and resists the idea that judgments which can be important in a child's life should depend on the subjective assessment of a teacher. Nevertheless, the decisive factor in achieving true quality of education is the teacher's awareness of quality and also his determination to aim for 'higher quality' in everything he does.

But the teacher is not there simply to *check* the pupils' actual attainment but also to *make sure* they reach it. That will find no favour with those who want to reduce the importance of the teacher and see him merely as an organiser of learning situations who provides material, creates suitable conditions for learning, accompanies, checks and assesses the learning process. That is correct to a limited extent, if one regards the school simply as a place of *training* where prescribed and assessable learning goals are to be achieved. But if one regards the school as a place of *education,* where every activity should be cultivated and thus raised to an aesthetic or even moral level, the teacher is, as ever, central to it: rooted in his endeavours to achieve true quality in his own life, he can set more far-reaching *goals*, choose the appropriate *methods and types of exercise* and be persistent in making the necessary *demands* on the students as a person they feel they can trust. Paper or the screen can at best be used to issue assignments, but children will only take demands that require real quality seriously *from a person* who means something to them.

'There cannot be two good teaching methods. There is only one good one and that is the one that rests entirely on the eternal laws of nature.'

3 Typical Pestalozzi

What is it actually that characterises Pestalozzi's theory of education?

Without a doubt it is the demand he repeated again and again that the work of education must be rooted in human nature.

Pestalozzi's view that human beings have a 'nature' — and an 'eternal, unchanging' one at that — is a source of dispute among philosophers. It can be objected that people are subject to social change and ultimately become what they make of themselves under the prevailing conditions. That can be seen from a simple comparison with animals. For example the life of the honey bee follows exactly the same course in the bee colony as two thousand years ago and it will still do so in two thousand years' time. It is, therefore, sufficient to study a single hive to know what the life of *the* bee is like, that is, what the nature of the bee is. It is quite different with human beings. Not only is the life of each individual different from that of all the others, but people live, and have always lived, in differing social systems, which will continue to change in the future. That appears to substantiate the hypothesis that there is nothing permanent in mankind, everything is changeable depending on the prevailing social conditions; and therefore, the hypothesis continues, basically everything is feasible in education as well.

But Pestalozzi resolutely opposed such a view. He was convinced that, despite the constant mutation of social conditions, there was something unchanging, eternal in human beings, something that remained true through *all* social change. Thus we all, wherever, whenever and however we live, have our physical and psychological needs. We are

17

all equipped with physical and mental faculties. We must all come to terms with our own egoism and suffer accordingly from the restrictions of society. And only after we have found and realised our life's task, which is beyond egoism, can we lead a truly fulfilled life (Pestalozzi calls this 'morality', 'becoming moral'.) And we are all endowed with a 'higher nature' as well, which is what makes this life in love and truth possible and allows us to see life as meaningful. Pestalozzi brings all these unchanging, eternal aspects together in the concept of *human nature*.

But it was also Pestalozzi's conviction that human nature is such that individuals cannot realise their true potential as *human beings* without the influence of other people. If people were simply left to themselves as they grew up, they would run wild. Pestalozzi often refers to the entirety of measures by which the forces of education of the time act on the child as *the art of education*, mostly, however, just as 'art'. Thus he says, 'Human beings only become human beings through art.' Since 'art' normally has a quite different meaning, Pestalozzi is often misunderstood.

There are, therefore, two 'forces' confronting each other in the development of every person, on the one hand unchanging human nature in its individual form, on the other *art*, which varies according to the social situation.

That raises the question of which of these two forces should take precedence. For Pestalozzi there is no possible doubt: nature has absolute precedence. In fact that is only logical since, if nature is unchanging but art can vary, art must be guided by nature. Thus Pestalozzi insists that art must *submit* to nature, that education and upbringing in general must be *in accord with nature* if people are to achieve the goal of full humanity.

This insistence rests, among other things, on his conviction that in a way the *ideal*, full humanity, is an undeveloped seed *within each individual's human nature*. This distinguishes Pestalozzi from those who see a person at birth metaphorically as a completely blank sheet of paper and consequently believe one can make anything one wants out of him. According to Pestalozzi, education should not *put things into* a person, but *develop* something within him and *bring it out*, namely full humanity.

The demand that education should be *in accord with human nature* is the absolute fundament of Pestalozzi's theory of education. Every further demand is nothing other than a specific clarification of this first, basic demand. Anything asked of a child which goes against its nature, will deform it and lead it away from the ultimate goal of education: full humanity.

Thus the very first requirement for a teacher who wants to teach and educate in the spirit of Pestalozzi is to ask himself at every turn: *Does what I am aiming for, what I am doing, what I ask the children to do, what I forbid them to do, correspond to the children's nature, is it in accord with human nature?*

That means that it is incumbent on the teacher to constantly improve his understanding of human nature. Pestalozzi called himself an 'authority on human nature' and as such he came to the conviction that individuals are not simply given the task of realising their full humanity but that nature has equipped them with the necessary *powers and faculties.* At birth these are still undeveloped and it is the task of the school and the home to support them in the *development of their powers and faculties.*

However, in this demand for the *development of powers and faculties,* hereditary factors, which can lead to differing talents, are only of secondary importance for Pestalozzi; what he understands first and foremost by 'powers and faculties' are those general human faculties which allow the individual to recognise the truth, make rational judgments, feel love that comes from the heart, experience religious faith and pursue all his affairs with vigour — that is to enjoy full humanity. But these powers are present in every individual in slightly different degrees, with the result that each person should realise his life's goal — full humanity — in his own way. Education can only be successful when it takes account of the unique, individual qualities in every student. (To avoid unrealistic demands on teachers by parents, I must point out that it is a misunderstanding to think that taking account of a pupil's individuality means granting his every wish and allowing each individual special rights. What it does mean is that teachers should be aware of what each pupil is capable of achieving, of his own special talents and should react spontaneously to his performance and his behaviour.)

As regards the potential for development of these powers and faculties, Pestalozzi is an optimist. He is convinced that the powers and faculties of each individual have an innate urge to develop. Thus he writes in his last important book, *Schwanengesang* (Swansong, 1825): *The nature of these faculties within each person drives him to use them. The eye wants to see, the ear to hear, the foot wants to walk and the hand to grasp. And, equally, the heart wants to believe and love, the mind wants to think. There is in every faculty of human nature an urge to rise from its inert, unskilled state to become a trained power.*

The aim for the teacher, therefore, is to encourage these faculties in their urge to develop, that is, to give them a helping hand. Results would be better in all our schools if teachers employed (and were allowed by the authorities to employ) and fostered first and foremost those activities which the pupils *want* to tackle — or at least are happy to tackle when we suggest them. Of course, to do this we would have to abandon the idea that all children must learn the same things, must always do the same things and must achieve the same goals. Despite that, all the basic requirements would be fulfilled because, in an atmosphere in which they feel their efforts are taken seriously, the children will stimulate and help each other, and be willing to accept stimulation from the teacher. I am well aware that this will make great demands on the teacher's competence as a teacher and that the organisation of the children in year-groups is not the ideal form for such an approach. Moreover, I am also aware that there are children who, as a result of poor upbringing on the part of their parents, are so spoilt or unruly that they would scarcely be able to take advantage of the freedom described here and thus provide support for all the arguments for tight control.

As an 'authority on human nature', Pestalozzi frequently expounded the view that human nature is not a single, harmonious whole. From the very beginning it is marked by tension and contradictions: our 'sensual, animal nature', which seeks pleasure and tries to avoid pain, confronts our 'higher, eternal, divine, inner' nature which enables the individual to enjoy a life of fulfilment in truth and love. While Pestalozzi believed that our 'animal nature' is the fundament of human existence, he was convinced that the individual can only know true fulfilment when our 'higher nature' receives its due and keeps the selfishness inherent in our animal nature within bounds. This Pestalozzi calls 'morality'.

In practice, the question that naturally arises is: How can I tell if what I am doing with the children is in accord with human nature?

There is one simple rule: teaching is in accord with human nature when the pupils throw themselves into their tasks with enjoyment. When that happens, hardly any conflict arises between pupils, or between the teacher and pupils. When, on the other hand, the children react against a topic or a particular teaching method or in a particular situation, are unwilling to learn or get distracted, that is usually a sign that the teaching is not in accord with human nature.

This last statement is likely to irritate teachers who take great pains in choosing and preparing topics and the means of putting them across, only to find that they still fail to get through to especially difficult children. It is quite understandable that they would reject the criticism that they were ignoring the principle of teaching in accord with human nature.

The answer from Pestalozzi's point of view would be that it is most likely that the previous education of these children had not been in accord with their nature and that consequently lessons which are successful for the general run of pupils are not in accord with the nature of *these children*. One could compare such a teacher with a doctor: if his tried and tested medicines prove ineffective, he does not look for a reason for their failure in the patient, simply in order to prove to himself that his treatment is correct; on the contrary, he tries different medicines and therapies. Similarly it is *pointless* (if understandable) for a teacher to cite the way children have been neglected and spoilt in order to justify his own methods. The failure is evident and leaves us with two alternatives: either we accept it, with all the consequences for the children concerned, for the class and the teacher, or we seek the course that is true to human nature, even in this difficult situation. In that case, to educate in accord with human nature means to accept *the nature of the specific child*, however twisted and messed-up it might appear to be, as a fact in which everything else must be grounded. And then it does indeed sometimes turn out that school, with some or all of its constituents and constraints (a particular teacher, with his particular style of communication and teaching, a specific class group, the demands of the timetable, specific methods, more general conditions such as the size of the school, things that happen on the way to school etc.) does indeed go directly against the natural needs of a difficult child. The reasons for compulsory education make sense, but we must never forget that this compulsion comes at a price and — unfortunately — claims its victims. Often enough there is no other solution but to collaborate with the parents, authorities and psychologists in looking for pragmatic solutions, in which we preserve as much that is in accord with the child's nature as possible, while accepting the regrettable, if necessary, restrictions on it. To abandon the idea of education in accord with a child's nature, however, and to seek a solution in measures which ignore it, is definitely going down the wrong route.

'Accord with human nature' has many different aspects and consequently there are often several reasons why pupils may sometimes join in with gusto and at others be unwilling to learn. Here I will limit myself to two examples of going against the principle of teaching in accord with human nature:

Choosing a topic or teaching method that is not appropriate for the age of the pupils. Very often our syllabuses and teaching materials, or inexperienced teachers, expect pupils to cope with topics or approaches which mean nothing to them or in which they have no real interest. The younger the children are, the more concrete, tangible, immediate a topic must be. Unfortunately this principle is often not observed. Thus in mathematics, children are often introduced to abstract formulae far too soon, when they cannot see their relevance for practical applications. Or in language classes pupils are burdened with ideas from linguistic theory at much too early an age, instead of being encouraged to discover the richness of language, the joy of speaking correctly, of writing fluently through exercises appropriate for children of their age. Or in history classes they find themselves confronted with political and sociological ideas and expected to pursue all kinds of research of their own, instead of being introduced to the lives of people in past ages through vivid, exciting stories or films, which will awaken their interest in historical events and processes. In geography they are expected to interpret statistical tables and explain global phenomena, instead of first of all being made familiar with the variety of landscapes and the people who inhabit them through stories, pictures, videos or, if possible, outings and trips. And biology classes often deal with molecular biology, genetics and biochemistry at an age when the children ought to start by looking at a flower, getting to know the most frequent plants or observing an animal, getting to know it and studying its behaviour.

Over-emphasis on the pupils' future needs. It is especially non-teachers who, when dealing with educational matters, tend to this one-sided view. Naturally schools have the task of preparing children for adult life. But that is not done by seeing in them primarily the future adults, but by responding to their *present needs and their present psychological state.* Much of what has to be done in school has to be done because the child needs it *at that point* for his healthy development. Taking a child's present state seriously is to nourish him psychologically and mentally.

I would like to give an example to illustrate this: the treatment of the fairy tale 'Hans in Luck' at infant level. The plot is simple: after serving his seven-year apprenticeship Hans is paid with a 'lump of silver as big as his head'. But he immediately exchanges it for a horse, that for a cow, the cow for a pig, the pig for a goose and the goose for a grindstone. With every exchange he feels happier and more fortunate than ever, and he feels happiest and most fortunate when he has got rid of everything. While it is true that the child will profit from this in terms of language learning — development of reading skills, expression, vocabulary and spelling — that alone does not justify dealing with Grimms' fairy tales. A sensitive teacher knows that *at this stage* children inhabit a world of images, which is reflected in the symbols of myths and dreams, and for that reason need the nourishment of such fairy tales. At that age a child is receptive to profound truths, as long as they are not presented in abstract, rational terms as moral instruction, but in living images. Without it needing to be pointed out explicitly, a child is quite capable of seeing in Hans simply a human being who has acquired a worldly treasure through hard work and faithfulness. But at the same time this lump of silver is the symbol of an inner treasure — the knowledge of the relativity of earthly riches. By responding fully to the true needs of each moment, and thus unburdening himself more and more of material possessions, he finds inner freedom, true fortune and happiness.

If schools were to concentrate solely on the things the majority of students are actually going to need in later life, we could presumably leave out drawing, writing stories, singing and looking at poems. We could also manage without most of the subject area of Man and the Environment, since in general grown-ups either ignore or forget these matters. And, anyway, much of what is needed for life is learnt outside school. If, despite all that, we as teachers continue to deal with this material, it is because the children need it *now* and by working with them in the right way can develop the faculties which are essential to enable them to live the life of a full human being such as Pestalozzi had in mind.

'The aim of education is the moral wholeness of our nature; its means are practice in striving for wholeness in moral behaviour, feeling and action.'

'Oh, come on,
4 everything's relative!'

One cannot talk about improving quality if one is afraid of making value judgments and demanding higher standards. That requires courage — especially today — and for several reasons.

Firstly: Once one starts discussing values, disagreements quickly arise. The philosophical argument revolves round the basic question: are there *objective* values by which we are bound, or are values on the one hand *socially defined* and on the other the result of *subjective* decisions by the individual? Neither of these two viewpoints can actually be proved. Ultimately they are a question of one's basic outlook. I myself tend towards the first position, without denying the fact that many value concepts are subject to both social change and subjective decisions. I prefer, however, to refer to standards of behaviour that change with society as 'norms' and regard them as socially determined realisations of objective values, which are fairly abstract and general, for example truth, goodness, beauty and holiness.

Secondly: There has never been agreement as to which values should be regarded as binding on us. Given this, the current attitude is to avoid any value judgments whatsoever. Thus the demand is often made that teaching in school should be value-free. But in the context of education, of teaching and instruction, the demand that we refrain from evaluation is a sheer impossibility; it ties the teacher's hands and leaves him unsure of himself: the things he 'feels' are wrong, could just as well be right; what 'seems' ugly to him, might be judged beautiful by another; what he 'regards' as bad, another might accept as good. The best solution appears to be to let the child 'decide' and to accept everything he says as good. But that is no help to the child; at best it leaves him revolving round himself, at worst it abandons him to neglect and indiscipline.

This dilemma is a problem for many teachers, who often find themselves being criticised for their belief in value judgments. My view is that education is only possible if we evaluate what a pupil says and does, and base appropriate demands and goals on that. It follows that the only people who are suited to this task are those who are prepared to make value judgments in their professional activity. People who are thus suited to the profession of teacher will no more be able to justify their values as universally binding than any philosopher, but they will be prepared to demonstrate these values in their own lives, to stand up for them to the children and their parents and not be afraid to risk conflict.

Thirdly: One reason why making judgments has fallen into disrepute is that there are situations in which it is unnecessary, indeed counterproductive. It is really tedious when one person insists on passing judgment on all decisions that belong to another's area of authority.

But the solution is not to refrain from value judgments. What is necessary is to draw clear distinctions. In my view there are two situations in which it is necessary to pass judgment: in the first place when one is *responsible* for the matter in question and in the second when *one's own wishes and needs* are affected. In all other cases passing judgment is unnecessary.

Accordingly, the teacher has the right and the duty to judge his pupils' behaviour and work, for there is no doubt that he bears a considerable share of responsibility for them. And his judgment is always called for when a pupil's behaviour affects him directly. He is in no way obliged to put up with any kind of insolence nor must he let disrespect of his work through all the well-known and tiresome disruption techniques pass without comment.

Fourthly: Making judgments can sometimes be difficult because one is afraid one might lose the pupil's affection. On school visits I often had the feeling the teacher was torn this way and that between his duty to achieve the goals formulated in the syllabus and a constant gnawing fear of alienating the children by making the necessary demands on them. Such teachers tended to accept almost anything from the children. They had become accustomed to responding to every contribution from their pupils with 'good', 'fine' or 'excellent', but often glanced only briefly at what they were being shown. A teacher who reacts to his pupils and their work in this way should not be surprised if his responses are not taken seriously. A relationship can only really be called good when weaknesses and shortcomings can come out into the open and be discussed in a tone that shows the pupil he is accepted.

Fifthly: Finally, many teachers find it difficult to confront their pupils with real aims and demands because they believe everything they are to learn and achieve should come from within them: spontaneity, creativity, self-realisation and imagination are highly thought of at the moment. This is quite rightly so, as long as one sees spontaneous impulses from the child as *one* side of the educational process; but we can only talk of real education when the *other side* is given its due. In order to develop fully as a human being, the growing individual needs to be forced to come to terms with social demands and to deal with products of human culture. And neither ability comes from within the child, they are represented in the aims and demands of school. These are laid down in the syllabuses and class attainment targets. As teachers, it is our duty to present these to our pupils and to make the products of human culture accessible to them.

Naturally that brings us into conflict with the current mood of our students. It is quite normal that they should want to find pleasure in what they do and avoid pain. If, however, we make this purely selfish pleasure principle an absolute, we are neglecting and betraying our mission, which is to support young people on their road to full humanity. We ought, rather, to be helping them to base their behaviour on a stable system of values instead of on their momentary need for pleasure. Both living as part of a community, a society, and a truly fulfilled personal life are only possible with this as a basis. And the students should find again and again that their pleasure in realising human values more than compensates them for any sacrifice of an agreeable moment they may have to make.

29

After all these considerations my advice is not to try to square the circle. As a teacher one has not merely the right, but also the duty to make demands and set goals. From that point of view, not everything the pupils produce is 'good', 'fine' or 'excellent'. Only once they have become keen to find out whether their work has been judged 'good' or 'slovenly and superficial' will they relate those words to their work and take them seriously, instead of simply trying to engage the teacher's attention. That, however, demands that one really goes into every piece of work the student produces and evaluates it according to what he is capable of producing. Only then can one give him an appropriate response, but it will be one that will have a positive effect on subsequent pieces of work.

'The whole range of instruction for young people should be designed more to develop faculties than to enrich knowledge.'

5 'Make an effort!'

When I was teaching at primary school there was a brickyard in the neighbouring village which gave me modelling clay to use in class and also fired the products — masks, pots — in their kilns free of charge. Once there was a disaster: the pots had obviously absorbed some moisture at the brickyard before being fired and they all fell to pieces and had to be thrown away. This was a wasted effort, then.

Really?

Let's check with Pestalozzi. As mentioned in chapter 3, he regards the development of powers and faculties as the basic task of education. If this is accepted, it brings us to the question of the *means* to achieve this. According to Pestalozzi, it comes about *entirely through children using their faculties*. They can only develop insofar as they are *active themselves*.

As far as the body is concerned, this principle of developing through activity is immediately obvious. We can talk as much as we like about the wonderful abilities of the human hand or the whole body, it will do nothing to develop strength, suppleness and dexterity. In the same way our mental and psychological faculties only develop through use. Pestalozzi emphasises this:

But the basic natural development of each of these individual faculties only comes about through its use. Love and faith, the fundament of our moral being, only develop naturally through the fact of love and faith themselves. And as human beings we only naturally develop the fundament of our mental faculties, thinking, through the fact of thinking itself. In the same way we only naturally develop the physical fundament of the faculties we need in our work, our senses, organs and limbs, through the fact of their use.

'Using one's faculties' means 'doing work'. If we look at this more closely, we can see that there is a dual aspect to the word 'work'. On the one hand it denotes a *result*, the *product* of an effort; on the other it denotes the effort itself, the process. In the economy it is the aspect of work as *product* that is emphasised, and justifiably so, since producing is its function. In the schools, on the other hand, nothing is produced; faculties are developed and therefore it is the aspect of work as *process* that is central. *The activity itself* is the essential, not the product that happens to come out of it. Thus the work of a potter, whose livelihood it is, is *pointless*, if the firing goes wrong. If, on the other hand, the pots made by the pupils suffer the same fate, their work was still meaningful, for the point of handicraft was not to produce pots, but to develop manual dexterity and a sense of form, and that was not lost, even though the pots broke.

That is not to say that the results of pupils' activities are unimportant. But the value of these results is not in themselves — as it is in economic production — but comes from their relationship to the process. Thus, for example, we are quite right to insist that exercise books and worksheets be kept neat and tidy — but not so that they will sell better. Rather, the requirement adds a presentational dimension to pupils' tasks, and neatly kept exercise books are visible evidence that they have been through the process in the desired way. And we must not forget that as a rule, pupils derive pleasure from a piece of work that has turned out well. This helps to create an atmosphere conducive to learning and is a motivation to continue making an effort. Thus visible products, factual knowledge and the mastery of certain skills all have their place within a system that understands education as a process.

Pestalozzi's concern that learning should first and foremost be a matter of developing faculties can be made clearer in the contrast between what some theories call 'material' and 'formal' education. 'Material education' is directed towards specific goals, that is, towards acquiring clearly defined knowledge and specific skills. Meanwhile, 'formal education' is more generally aimed at extending the pupil's range of possible responses that comes from dealing with specific goals, which are thus a *means to the end* of developing faculties. There is no topic that cannot be used to encourage the general development of faculties. What is essential is that we as teachers bear the 'formal education' aspect in mind when dealing with a specific topic. Therefore when reviewing a lesson we must ask ourselves: Did the pupils really make progress? Were the demands made on their faculties such that they were strengthened and such that the range of possibilities available to them were extended? Which faculties were they? And did all pupils profit from this?

In my capacity as a teacher trainer I found it fairly easy to see, during school visits, whether the faculties and natural abilities of the pupils were being engaged: no development of faculties in Pestalozzi's sense was taking place if the pupils were fooling around with their neighbours, if they weren't concentrating, if they worked in a hurried, slapdash way to get the task over with as soon as possible. When the children's faculties really are active, everything looks different: they are all concentrating on their work, the atmosphere is calm, the only talk is related to the topic and the task, the pupils do not want to be disturbed and distracted from their work. And if the teacher has to leave the room for any reason, chaos does not immediately break out, it remains as quiet as before, the pupils continue to concentrate on their work as if nothing special had happened. I have frequently seen children react with irritation when the school bell rang and they had to break off from their work.

'If only,' is what some of you will be thinking. As teachers we are well aware of the many ways pupils have of resisting, which brings us to the question: What *means* are available to the teacher to get the pupils to produce real work?

The most widespread means is psychological pressure, usually with the help of the assessment system. That is understandable because we teachers are ourselves under pressure to succeed — under a quite particular kind of pressure: our success, as accepted by society, is only indirectly dependent on us, but directly dependent on the behaviour of our pupils. When our *pupils* achieve good results and behave in an acceptable manner, *we* are assessed as being good teachers.

However widespread, however obvious psychological pressure may be as a means to motivate pupils, it is, in the final analysis, counterproductive. No one likes pressure and so the pupils respond with counter-pressure, with the end result that they come to regard any kind of learning or effort as something to be avoided as far as possible and quite naturally put the responsibility for their progress onto the teacher. It would be naive to ignore this.

What should our goal be? It must be to get the pupils to *enjoy* work. Pestalozzi puts it succinctly: *'No amount of learning is worth a penny if it suppresses enjoyment and motivation.'* That pupils can do good work and enjoy it can be seen not only in the many classrooms where that happens, but also in the area of leisure activities. Many go riding, play football in a club, go to ballet class — and, lo and behold, they are often happy to accept any kind of effort it takes.

Why does this not work just as well in school? There are many reasons. Successful teaching is often rendered impossible by the resentment and recalcitrance of difficult pupils who have not learnt to be obedient, to commit themselves to something or to curb their own egoism. All coercion, everything which reduces individual freedom, consequently everything that is obligatory, can lessen the enjoyment of work: compulsory schooling, being forced to be part of a community, the timetable, the curriculum, prescribed attainment targets. Everything that causes fear can detract from the enjoyment: pressure from parents and teachers, the assessment system, fear of failing exams, fear of failing in front of one's classmates. Anyone who is unable to refute this is bound to agree that our school system, which is increasingly organised down to the very last detail and increasingly reduces the freedom that is essential for education to take place, is not the answer.

But despite all these impediments, experience shows that under certain conditions it is possible to create an atmosphere that is conducive to learning. The main means of achieving this are: *love of children, leading by example, recognising their individuality, encouraging them and engaging with them in their work.* The antagonism between teachers and pupils, which we come across all too often, must be replaced by an all-round sense of togetherness. Pupils who realise the teacher is on their side gradually abandon their resistance and become willing to be involved in a process of learning and development which is to the benefit of all. I would emphasise that there are no easy solutions; everything must be taken as a whole, everything is interconnected — and seen in that light, each single chapter of this book is designed to show how, despite everything, pupils can be persuaded to enjoy work.

'Knowledge is of little worth for a human being, familiarisation is everything.'

6 On Manners and Other Values

Reliability, thoroughness, perseverance, orderliness, cleanliness, carefulness, love of detail, decency, prudence, conscientiousness, politeness, respect, discipline.

These represent a whole cluster of traditional values and some people might feel very uncomfortable at the thought of them. But the quality of education will not improve until we start living our lives according to them once more.

Naturally a world in which *these* values are the only ones recognised and are imposed by *force* would be a sterile world and therefore repulsive to us. We should put the question the other way round: *Is the state of affairs that arises when these values are neglected acceptable, even desirable?* One only needs to visualise a chaotic world full of disorder, with nothing but unreliable, superficial, impolite and grubby people who have nothing to hold on to and lack even a minimum of decency. Surely no one can seriously want that?

So let me state the obvious: the whole quality of schools will improve if we require both ourselves and the pupils to observe the rules properly, keep to agreed times, do each piece of work with the requisite thoroughness and care, be attentive and polite to each other, keep ourselves and our clothes neat and tidy, and avoid unnecessary and excessive noise. That will give the learning community — that is the class — qualities such as discipline, seriousness, stability, an agreed set of values. As long as we treat everything as of equal value, if not as a matter of indifference, as long as everything is arbitrary, lacking direction, as long as any uncontrolled outburst is tolerated — as long as that is the situation we will lack the atmosphere that is conducive to true education.

At this point I hear the first objection: Do creativity, imagination, spontaneity mean nothing to you? And my answer? They mean a lot to me, such a lot, in fact, that I want to create the conditions in which they can be expressed *genuinely, not just for outward show*. I do not accept that people are more creative the greater the disorder and noise surrounding them, the more casual their behaviour towards others and the less they stick to any agreements they have made.

And the second objection follows immediately: Your peace and quiet, your order, reliability, carefulness, punctuality, politeness and thoroughness are just empty forms with no content, imposed on people, mere externals, with no inherent value of their own.

That is a point worth discussing. First of all I will have to go into the twin concepts of form and content, which have occupied philosophers for centuries. 'Content' refers to expressions of the creative spirit such as works of art, scientific discoveries, lawmaking, displays of power, playful behaviour, but also to material products. The more farseeing, intuitive, sensitive and creative the mind that produces these contents is, the weightier the products one leaves behind will be.

But we can only deal with these contents because they are all realised in some *form*. 'Content' never appears without assuming 'form'. If we want to explore any content we have to engage with the form. Content without form is inconceivable.

Unfortunately the reverse is not true. Form without content is very conceivable. We see it in everyday life: someone's manners are perfect but void of meaning, hypocritical; the painting has fluent brushstrokes but when one takes a closer look all they conceal is emptiness; rules are followed, but they do nothing for our lives; the system works, only no one knows what its purpose is; the custom is observed, but the idea behind it has gone; prayers are said, songs sung, maxims quoted, but it's all empty words.

However contradictory it sounds, the fact is that content seeks form, but forms tend to eat up their content, leaving behind empty shells, which take up excessive space, demonstrate great force of inertia and cut off large areas, drained of meaning, from new life.

40

But it is taking our scepticism regarding forms too far to refuse to acknowledge the need for their existence. What we must do is to check how genuine they are, how justified, how necessary and how far they match the content that goes with them. Forms must always be examined to see how adequately they perform their task of 'containing' content. But if we discern a disparity between form and content, rejecting form as such is not the answer. What we are faced with is the choice between two positive, equally valid possibilities: either we return the original content to its form or we look for new forms which will adequately present the desired content. Formlessness is not a solution.

When talking of 'form' and 'content', the duality of 'external' and 'internal' appears almost automatically, although of course it would not be correct to see the two pairs as the same. Nowadays there is a widely held view that externals are only justified when they are founded on something internal, on a person's inner life, on their firm convictions, otherwise the behaviour is a sham. The slogan is: First of all feel thankful, then express your thanks; first of all be in a cheerful mood, then sing your song; first of all be in a peaceable frame of mind, then shake your neighbour by the hand; first of all feel genuine interest, then open the book; first of all believe, then pray or go to church.

I, too, think that this is the ideal way. If we can get our pupils to calm down inside, they will go about their work, their play, their learning calmly; if we can teach our pupils to appreciate the value of keeping their thoughts in order, we will find it easier to keep order in class; if we develop respect for their fellows in our pupils, they will behave politely and considerately towards each other; if we can encourage them to treat objects with care, they will be pleased when they produce a neat and tidy piece of work; if we can open their eyes to the beauty of plants, animals and the countryside, they will protect them and not leave litter lying about; if we can teach them to love the truth, they will be prepared to do everything they undertake thoroughly and conscientiously. It is easy to write these things, but the experienced teacher will also see their illusory aspect.

It is therefore worth asking whether the reverse might not be effective. Does a small child not gradually develop a sense of gratitude from being told simply to say 'thank you' every time it is given a helping hand? Do we not learn to order our thoughts when we are trained to keep all our screws, all our pencils, all our books together? Does an appreciation of the aesthetic not develop over time if we are required to write neatly, set out our written work carefully, speak clearly and with expression and to look after our things? Do we not slowly calm down when we simply remain silent for a while? Does our depression not gradually go away when we make an effort and join others in some game? All these cases start out — some perhaps only ostensibly — from the externals and the internal development follows.

Both of these ways are familiar from psychotherapy: depth psychologists hope that the resolution of inner conflicts will lead to changes in behaviour; behavioural therapy works 'from outside', on visible behaviours, on what depth psychologists regard as symptoms. While it is true that the proponents of these two theories are at loggerheads, both have successes to show.

And it was in his very first writing on education, the Stans Letter, that Pestalozzi himself recognised, on the basis of his experiences, the particular effectiveness for education of 'accustoming a child to the mere posture of a virtuous life.' Thus he wrote, after he had described how he had aroused the children's sympathy for refugees from the war: *Furthermore, I linked these feelings to exercises in self-control so that they could use them to achieve discipline in their lives. In this respect organised discipline in the institution was not possible. That, too, was to develop step by step as needs became apparent. Quiet as a means of encouraging the children's activity is perhaps the first secret of such an institution. The quiet I demanded when I was there and teaching was a great help towards achieving my goal, as was the insistence on the physical posture in which they had to sit... Amongst other things I told them, as a joke, to keep their eyes on their big finger when they were repeating what I had said. It is incredible how the insistence on such little details can give the teacher the basis for great ends. No one would believe, unless they had seen it, how a girl that has been allowed to run wild takes a first step on the road of moral development simply by becoming accustomed to holding her body and head straight for hours on end without letting her gaze wander. These experiences have taught me that accustoming a child to the mere posture of a virtuous life can make an immeasurably greater contribution to the real development of an ability to behave virtuously than any number of lectures and sermons, which do nothing to further this behaviour. Also, by following this principle my children were clearly more serene, calmer, more open to everything that is noble and good than one would have supposed from the complete absence of any concept of goodness in their heads... I explained very little to my children; I taught them neither religion nor morality; but when they were so quiet that you could hear every breath, I asked them, 'Aren't you more sensible and better when you're like this than when you're making a racket?'*

Of course, it would be inappropriate to try and imitate Pestalozzi in any specific detail, since his day our lifestyle has changed considerably in many respects. What is important is the fundamental insight that mind and behaviour, interior and exterior, content and form are in a living relationship and *interact* with each other. It is, therefore, always worth trying both ways: to affect the exterior through the interior and the interior though the exterior.

To illustrate my idea I would like to recount a little episode, which took place while I was teaching:

It is winter, half past seven in the morning and therefore still dark. The sixteen-year-old trainee teachers are sitting in a circle with me and I ask them to start by singing Martin Luther's hymn 'Ev'ry morning, fresh and true/ The Lord outpours His grace anew.' I give the note, bring them in and let the class sing. It's awful. Nothing 'fresh' about it at all, morose rather, at best apathetic, not the least commitment. They just about manage to keep going until the final note. I had foreseen that it would be like that. Then, sitting up straight in my chair and trying to look 'fresh' myself, I said something along the lines of, 'No, not like that. Now would you please all sit up straight, breathe in together, sing loud enough for everyone to hear, think of the words of the hymn and try as hard as you can to sing a cheerful morning song.' Then I brought them in with a flourish, conducted them with gusto, and the hymn rang out such that it was a joy to hear. Then I drew the conclusion I had been aiming at from the start: 'The first time we all sang the way we felt. Who likes to get up this early in winter to go to school? And if they have to, who feels like singing a morning song? If I were to regard our mood as an absolute, I would have to say, we can't help it, our psychological state won't let us sing it any other way. But as the example has shown, we could sing it another way thirty seconds later. It is the difference between the first and the second time we sang the hymn that is important, *for that is the precise measure of our freedom.'*

Let us return to the values I mentioned at the start of this chapter. Each of them lays an obligation on us — both teachers and pupils — but they also give us a certain measure of freedom, which depends on our understanding and our good will. If we neglect these values, learning will suffer. The pupils as well as the teacher will expend much too much energy on things that have nothing to do with the topic, for problems and conflicts will constantly arise. If the attitudes and behaviour associated with these values are imposed by force, are mere external form that is, then something is wrong. But if one abandons them because of that, things are even more wrong. The only possible solution is to make them a permanent part of one's teaching, to try and fill them with content, with life, by one's own example and, of course, by discussion and exhortation as well. Then they will no longer be mere externals, void of meaning, but an expression of true humanity and contribute to an atmosphere in which committed, fruitful learning can take place.

'Only something that can take hold of a person in the power of his common humanity, that is as heart, mind and hand, really and truly forms him according to nature.'

7 **The Famous Trinity**

Here in Switzerland people mostly know two things about the great philosopher and best-known Swiss, Heinrich Pestalozzi: in the first place he was a simpleton because he would give away the shirt off his back ('I'm not Pestalozzi' is a phrase that is generally even today understood in Switzerland), and in the second he was perpetually muttering 'Head, heart and hand' to himself all the time.

Joking aside, Pestalozzi did indeed take the famous trinity as his guideline when he wrote about people, their potential, their upbringing and education. We find it articulated in hundreds of sentences, but it is also used to order his thoughts in wider contexts. He does not always use the same words, but varies his vocabulary, though in such a way that the gist of what he is saying is always clear. The precise sequence 'head, heart and hand' occurs only once in the forty-five volumes of his writings, in his argument with the Prussian pastor, Karl Heinrich Gottfried Witte. It was about the question of whether Pestalozzi's ideas on elementary education were suitable for the poor alone or for all people. For Pestalozzi the answer was clear: his 'method' was equally valid for poor and rich because it corresponded to human nature.

This view incurred the hostility of many nobles. On the one hand they felt that for the poor such education went too far, and on the other not far enough for the rich. Pestalozzi found this outrageous: *It would be taking people too far, would it, if the poor of the country were helped in a way that is in accord with human nature, if they were enabled to become, with head, heart and hand, what all people in the country ought to be with head, heart and hand for God, themselves and their native land?*

Interesting in this respect is the final clause, in which Pestalozzi makes it clear *for whom* the individual ought to *be* a whole person: God, himself and his native land (i.e. society and the state).

Let us take a closer look at this famous trinity. As I have shown, Pestalozzi's basic concern as a teacher was to develop the child's natural faculties. Now clearly, we humans have very many and very varied powers and faculties at our disposal to shape our lives. Pestalozzi arranges them in three groups, following the division of the psyche into thought, feeling and action, that goes back to ancient Greece. This trinity is represented symbolically by the organs *head, heart and hand.*

Easiest to understand is what Pestalozzi means by 'head': all the psychological and intellectual functions that allow us to understand the world and form rational judgments about things. They include perception, memory, imagination, thought and language. Pestalozzi often refers to these faculties as 'mind', as 'mental' or 'intellectual' faculties.

More difficult is Pestalozzi's concept of 'heart'. By that he did not simply mean the diverse feelings that accompany our perceptions and thoughts, but first and foremost the basic moral feelings of love, faith, trust and gratitude, plus also the activity of our conscience, our sensing of beauty and goodness, the ordering of our lives according to moral values. Instead of 'heart' he often talks of basic 'moral-religious' or 'moral' faculties.

The area covered by 'hand' is also very complex. Pestalozzi often also calls this area 'physical faculties', 'manual faculties', 'faculties of art', 'faculties of profession', 'domestic faculties' or even 'social faculties'. What he has in mind with 'hand' is our practical activity in which manual dexterity and physical strength combine with common sense and will power in productive action.

It has to be admitted that, looked at from the point of view of logic, this arrangement is problematic. Pestalozzi was aware of this and in various places emphasised that when he talked of 'hand', for example, the intellectual faculties had to be included in the concept. Despite that, he stuck to the trinity and derived two basic demands from it: in the first place, none of the faculties were to be neglected, all should be developed to the full and in harmony; in the second, we must recognise and accept that each of these groups of faculties develops according to its own laws.

Notwithstanding that, Pestalozzi does not see all three groups as equal in value. It is only the *faculties of the heart* whose value he accepts unconditionally. Only these enable us to reach our true goal of full humanity. The faculties of head and hand do have to be developed as far as possible, but they are only beneficial to us insofar as we allow ourselves to be guided by our fully developed faculties of the heart in employing them. However intelligent or physically skilful anyone is, if they do not combine their intelligence and skill with a sense of responsibility, with the desire to do good and, wherever possible, with love, they will make themselves and other people unhappy.

At this point a short *digression* is necessary. Given the subject of this book, I continue to talk about 'heart', 'the heart's faculties', 'the development of the heart'. But there is something inside me resisting it, namely my awareness of how out-of-date these expressions are. As 'modern' people, we feel that talk of the 'heart' — as long as we don't mean our blood pump — is melodramatic, sentimental or even kitsch. It is certainly 'unscientific'. More acceptable would be 'affective faculty', 'emotive functions', only they do not express what is meant. For Pestalozzi, 'heart' means above all our moral faculty. But that does not get us much farther, since the question of whether morality is based on rational consideration or on impulses from our inner being is still a matter of debate. Pestalozzi is in no doubt that the basis of moral action is not the head, but the heart.

My way out of the dilemma is to point out that every concept, whether modern or out-of-date, is merely an attempt to make the ultimately unfathomable mystery of life available to our consciousness and thus allow us to talk about it. Every use of language rests on the unspoken agreement that the content one is formulating will only reach the other person insofar as the words and sentences used are able to arouse images and understanding *of their own* within them. Trusting that this is what will happen, I will continue to adhere to Pestalozzi's mode of expression, well aware of the problems associated with it.

The demand for harmonious education - that is for the development of all three groups of faculties - is fundamental for the teacher who wants to teach in the spirit of Pestalozzi. It is, of course, not possible to address all three groups every minute, for in some subjects the 'head' is central, in others the 'hand'. But in every case it is desirable and also, in principle, possible to bring the heart's faculties into play. A pupil who approaches lessons with keen interest, indeed enthusiasm, but also with consideration for his fellow pupils, will always be putting his 'heart' into his work. That is why Pestalozzi demands: Put your heart into everything! *Only when teacher and pupils put their hearts into teaching and learning can true education as Pestalozzi intends it take place.*

As indicated above, 'heart' does not simply equate to feeling. Fury, anger, hatred, boredom, displeasure, pain, depression — these are also feelings, but they are not included in what we understand by 'heart'. A person has 'heart' when the determining elements in their make-up are the 'moral emotions' such as sympathy, love, joy, gratitude. Such a person is always a good person. They have a rich inner life; they are sensitive and open to impressions; they appreciate beauty, the finer things of life; they are unreserved in their love of truth but do not reject absolute clarity of thought. They are people endowed with genuine reason, which they do not confuse with cold intellect.

Pestalozzi's insights encourage the teacher to appeal to the pupils' 'hearts' in everything that is done as part of learning. It is a good start if they keep *feeling a sense of wonderment*. Nowadays that is very difficult, given the way children are constantly bombarded with images and superficial knowledge. It is probably only possible when the teacher himself has not lost his own sense of wonderment and his pupils hold him in high regard. Then the children may even come to the point where they can feel *respect* when confronted with examples of the great, the sublime, and thus develop an attitude to life which is ultimately the basis on which men can build a fruitful life together.

One can always tell that the 'heart' is involved when the pupils are working with real pleasure. As is well known, teaching is not just a trade, it is an art. If a teacher has mastered it, he is able to teach with pleasure and to motivate the pupils to learn with pleasure. They feel this especially when they *achieve the goals that have been set* and thus *really get a sense of their own ability*. But that is only possible when they feel they are *accepted and loved* by their teacher and classmates. 'You're good — you can do it — we're all pleased when you make an effort and are successful' should run like a ground bass beneath all communication between teacher and pupils. Such a basic atmosphere is the opposite of the aggressiveness that often exists between pupils and teachers and to a large extent derives from a lack of mutual respect.

In everything that happens in school there should be a place for beauty, the pupils should be able to feel it. Learning 'with heart', combining respect, joy, friendship and beauty, can then gradually arouse in them a love of the things they undertake and perhaps also *love of life*.

The endeavour to develop all faculties harmoniously and to give priority to the heart's faculties has far-reaching consequences for schools. Whenever a teacher succeeds in approaching this Pestalozzian ideal, lessons become what one can accurately describe as an *experience*. If that occurs, pupils will learn out of genuine interest. They will no longer simply be trying to get a good mark, but will throw themselves into their task with head, hand and heart. The path that leads to the learning outcome will no longer be felt as tedious, but as exciting and fulfilling. The pupils will work hard and with commitment, and the conflicts between them, or with the teacher, which keep disturbing the class when the teaching is not in accord with their nature, will largely disappear.

'The schoolmaster based his teaching, designed to inculcate love in the children, not on making them listen to sayings about love and its blessings, and learning them by heart, but by putting love itself into practice.'

8 Preaching Morality?

'The school should be responsible for a child's *education*, that is the transfer of knowledge that is important for society, and the corresponding skills, the parents for their children's *upbringing*, that is seeing that they behave in a manner that is both moral and socially acceptable.' This is a frequently heard demand. From Pestalozzi's point of view that would mean the school is responsible for head and hand, the parents for the heart. This is impossible.

Every experienced teacher knows you cannot educate children properly without at the same time contributing to their upbringing; a lack of good upbringing hinders education. What we are aiming for is always what Pestalozzi calls the *forming of whole human beings*. Good teaching always includes manners and morals.

Thus contributing to *upbringing* — or, if you prefer, *moral education* — is one of our tasks as teachers. For we encounter morally deficient behaviour among the children on a daily basis: they reject a classmate, mock others unrestrainedly, trip them up, bully them during break or on the way home, steal, hit and kick out, lie without blushing, swear and use obscenities that would disgust any decent person. We cannot simply look away and calmly drink our coffee during break.

But what should we do? Tell them off? Encourage them to improve? The effects quickly wear off. Or punish them? That might make them behave, but it won't make them better people. Hardly have we turned our backs then they will be at it again. And a telling-off or a punishment is always a *reaction* to misbehaviour that has already taken place. It is — as Schleiermacher puts it — *counteractive* rather than *supportive*.

Now it is true that both counteraction and support are needed in moral education, but the second is the decisive factor. Our priority should not be to *suppress* morally deficient behaviour, but to *develop* moral behaviour. The more successful we are in this, the less we will need to take counteractive measures. It is not enough just to get the children not to hit each other, they should like each other, help each other, show commitment to the community and a love of truth. To achieve this we must — as Pestalozzi puts it — *develop their heart's faculties*. But the heart's faculties only develop through being used.

That brings us to the question of how, as teachers, we can activate these faculties in the children so that they will put their trust in others, show understanding, curb their selfishness and try to do good.

This cannot be done by pressure, coercion, force. I can shout as loud as I like at a pupil, telling him he can trust me, the more I do so the more he will shut himself off. However strong the threats with which I try to get him to love his classmates — he will do the opposite out of contrariness. Goodness cannot be brought about by force. Morality is always founded on a free decision of the individual.

The first effective means of moral education is the *example* set by the teacher. If I want my pupils to behave in a certain way, I must behave in that way myself. It starts with politeness in dealing with other people and continues from keeping your person, clothes and desk neat and tidy to being conscientious and thorough in doing your work and fulfilling your obligations. A teacher who has a wide range of interests, always insists on getting to the bottom of things, goes about his work cheerfully and takes care over it, will inspire his pupils to approach things in the same manner. But the decisive factor in all this is the relationship between a teacher and his pupils. If they have a good relationship emotionally, the pupils will be much readier to copy their teacher's behaviour. If not, they will not give a damn what he does.

Behaviour that can be observed can also be copied. But moral education goes deeper. We want to encourage our pupils to develop the *ethical foundations of their own morality*. As we have already indicated, that can only be achieved by stimulating the heart's faculties and that takes place according to the law of *resonance*. Living morality can only be aroused and encouraged in a person through seeing morality lived out in others — especially those involved in their upbringing. That is more than copying a model, it is being opened up by the teacher's essential nature.

This idea is so important to me that I would like to illustrate it by a comparison with the viola d'amore. This baroque instrument usually has seven main strings and seven 'sympathetic' strings below them. These are not played by the bow but start to sound when a note is played on the corresponding main string. This happens according to the law of *resonance* and gives the instrument its individual, sweet sound.

The opportunities open to those involved in a child's upbringing can be viewed in the light of this law. The strings that are bowed can symbolise the moral aspects of the teacher's life, the sympathetic strings those of the children. Just as the main string can only make the sympathetic string resonate by vibrating *itself*, we can only awaken a child's 'heart' through our *own* inner life.

In other words, love arouses love, respect fosters respect, trust creates a willingness to trust others, one's own openness opens up the children's hearts and minds, one's own sense of responsibility motivates the children to behave responsibly, one's own commitment to values encourages them to base their actions on values. Enthusiasm for work done in the normal course of teaching can arouse similar feelings in the pupils.

Resonance can also not occur, even though the string is played. That happens either when the corresponding sympathetic string is missing, or when it is blocked or when the medium by which the vibration is transmitted is missing; resonance does not occur in a vacuum.

This is also true in the metaphorical sense. It is possible that the teacher's efforts will set off little or no resonance in some pupils for the simple reason that the corresponding disposition is not there in the pupils or is not sufficiently developed. It is a mistake to assume that every person can be everything and that everyone can do everything whatever their age. To return to our image: just as a blocked sympathetic string remains mute, blockages in a pupil can prevent resonance: tiredness, lack of concentration, conflicts with classmates, unrequited love, problems at home, failures he has not yet come to terms with.

Finally, resonance can only arise when the two strings can vibrate in a medium surrounding both. In our context this medium is a positive, living *teacher-pupil relationship*. We could call it the fertile soil which is essential if education and development in the widest sense are to flourish. If this relationship is seriously disturbed, then the teacher's efforts, the methods he resorts to, will mostly be counterproductive. The more enthusiastic he is about his subject, the easier it is for hostile pupils to hurt him — they simply need to do nothing and describe the subject as sh... And all his moral exhortations will go in one ear and out the other.

It was Pestalozzi's conviction that living morality develops solely within interpersonal relationships. Thus he writes, *'Basically our species only develops true humanity face to face, heart to heart.'* It is, therefore, of decisive importance for a child's moral development for him to be part of a community which is marked by love, trust, consideration and understanding.

But despite this fundamental insight of Pestalozzi's, it is clear that resonance can also be created by the products of our culture such as books, music, songs, videos and computer games. They all bear the stamp of the human spirit, which works indirectly through the things it creates. Therefore we teachers must not only bear the significance of the teacher-pupil relationship and the class community in mind and make them a positive environment, but we must also consider the resonance that can be produced by those cultural products that fascinate our pupils. Of course, we have to recognise that unfortunately this includes much rubbish as well as much that is beneficial.

As we mentioned in the previous chapter, each of the three groups of faculties, head, heart and hand, develops according to its own laws. In the heart - that is in the area of moral education - Pestalozzi sees three stages.

The *first* stage is the awakening of a *sense of morality* within the child's inner being. This comes about according to the law of resonance, which we have been talking about. Pestalozzi often refers to this sympathetic vibration, this integration in the life of a community marked by love, as 'inner perception'.

In the *second* stage Pestalozzi demands *doing good* on the basis of *obedience*. Thus he himself encouraged the children in the orphanage in Stans to share their bread with starving children from Altdorf, letting them feel the consequences of a moral act by going short themselves.

Even today, a teacher can incorporate Pestalozzi's principles in his teaching by combining school learning with moral action. As an example I would like to mention a teacher who, together with his pupils, composes a message for each of the fortnightly pages of a calendar. The educational aspect of this is an intensive investigation into a topic that is of great importance for human life and in the children's own experience: water, wood and forests, houses, bridges, crossing frontiers. At the end of the year the pages are photocopied, made into wall calendars and sold. Part of the money made is always used for a project in one of the developing countries, for example digging a well. Thus the pupils not only learn about the importance of water, they are also involved in the production of the calendar with the sense that they are helping people in need.

Naturally not every topic studied at school can be combined with this kind of moral action. But anyone who is teaching in the spirit of Pestalozzi will constantly find ways of satisfying this requirement. There is one thing we must be clear about though: a teacher can only do this if his work with the class rests on genuine *authority*. Then the pupils' response will be obedience in the sense Pestalozzi means it: willing acceptance of what is good.

The *third* stage of moral education for Pestalozzi is *thinking and talking about what is good*. The idea is that pupils should not discuss moral laws until they have a feeling of what is good and have experienced what it means to do good. Otherwise, he says, all their talk would be nothing but empty prattle.

In class there will always be opportunities to discuss people's motives with the pupils, to examine them and decide to what extent they should be seen as morally estimable or reprehensible. This is particularly the case with *history* lessons, in which the pupils are constantly confronted with the actions of exceptional people who behaved in either an unscrupulous or a morally outstanding manner. The same is true of *reading*. Many stories show people having to decide between good and evil. Finally, *actual conflicts* within the class can provide scope for reflecting on the nature of moral action.

And now I must ask your forgiveness. I wanted to show that one could not get very far with ethical education by 'preaching morality'.

8 Preaching Morality?

And now I have done it myself — and not only here! But since I have started, I might as well go on. In fact the whole vision of the school that I am presenting here is really about morality. To have young people in our care for most of their childhood and youth and not to give them pleasure and help them find their true goal in life is lacking in morality. Perhaps the problems we have in education today are the same as those in the economy: it is all about efficiency, a quick profit, rationalised organisation and actual human beings, with their human needs, are often overlooked. In our hectic determination to reform education have we not lost sight of the basic truth, namely that education should not be designed first and foremost according to the needs of society, the economy and the state, but should aid children and young people to achieve full humanity?

'An animal is completely fitted for everything it needs to do; human beings are fitted for nothing but what they learn, practise and love.'

9 'A human being is only fully human when he is practising.'

Correct, the title is not from Schiller, for what he said was, 'A human being is only fully human when he is *playing*.' And that makes him more attractive to us than Herr Otto Friedrich von Bollnow, who altered the sentence in that clumsy manner. But Bollnow's version brings out two things: firstly, we only develop the skills which make a full life possible through practice; and secondly, proper practice has the lack of self-awareness that is part of true play.

Both — playing and practising oblivious to everything else — can be observed in children as one and the same thing. They forget themselves, time and the world around them, and are completely absorbed, without intention or self-reflection, in an activity that develops their faculties, broadens their mind and fills their whole being. Playing and practising are united.

Maria Montessori was once secretly observing a child of kindergarten age as it fitted ten rods of varying thickness into the matching holes in a board. Each time it had completed the task, it took them out, mixed them up and started from the beginning again. The child repeated the exercise over forty times, then breathed out as a sign of satisfaction and relief and went away. Its deep breath said, 'There, I can do that now.'

It is clear that the enjoyment of repeating a series of movements or an activity is part of a child's nature — and of that of human beings in general. An unspoilt child does it spontaneously, without being told to, simply from some inner urge. It does not know that it needs to do so for its development, but 'its nature' does. Practising, repeating something, losing oneself in some activity — that is absolutely in accord with human nature.

In their leisure activities some children are quite prepared to repeat certain things hundreds of times. One just has to go to a ballet lesson, observe a child trying to play a tune by ear on some instrument, watch young people going down steps on their rollerblades and skateboards, it is always the same: they try, try and try again until they can do it — and then they often raise the bar.

It is only at school that it doesn't seem to work like that! If a teacher gets his pupils to do a large number of similar sums, read a passage several times or keep conjugating verbs until they can do it without faltering, he will very quickly hear the criticism that they are mechanical drills. Drill — how soul-destroying! — it doesn't even have a place on the parade ground any more.

Nowadays we are going to great lengths in research, legislation, organisation and financial support to improve education, which is obviously seen as unsatisfactory. As someone working at the chalk face, one is tempted to make the subversive suggestion; 'How about bringing back more practice drills?'

It is easy to demand more practice, but there are clearly many aspects of the present situation which make it difficult for teachers actually to employ the technique.

I see *one reason* in the current dependence on *course materials*. Teaching is determined far more by teaching materials than by the syllabus. Whilst in the past coursebooks were written by experienced practising teachers, nowadays they are designed by specialists in educational science with a team of advisers. Their high degree of perfection suggests implicitly that they cover all the teaching goals within a subject area. But one can only achieve these goals if one adheres fairly strictly to the prescribed route through the course materials and that often leaves teachers very little scope for classroom activities of their own devising. These teaching materials do usually contain a scheme of exercises, perhaps even a book with exercises, but the sheer size of the package tends to mean the teacher is constantly under pressure. Above all, true practice demands that one be allowed to take one's time over it and that one can go into the *specific difficulties of the individual pupils*. But these are often not catered for by the teaching materials and therefore require additional exercises and additional time to go through them.

The *second reason* is connected with the first. It is a simple truth that nowadays *too much* is expected of schools as regards subjects, themes and topics in relation to the time allowed. Science is constantly opening up new areas of knowledge, and technical and social developments require more and more new skills. This means that the pressure on schools to 'modernise' becomes greater and greater. At the same time they are encouraged to jettison 'out-of-date' materials, but these are often the elementary foundations which have to be understood and mastered before pupils can make sense of new discoveries and techniques. In this situation, in which a high quality of material and work is demanded, it is the tried and tested method of taking the time to practise what has been taught that is sacrificed. Those who suffer most are the slower and less intelligent pupils.

The *organisation of education* is also a hindrance to regular practice. The system of using specialist subject teachers is becoming more and more widespread, even at the primary stage, and that reinforces the status of what Martin Wagenschein has called 'putting the pupils through the forty-five-minute mincer'. But this way of dividing up the pupils' daily learning time is anything but natural; on the contrary, it is highly artificial and does not correspond to their psychology. It is only when one can forget time and everything around that one can get close to the essence of what one is dealing with. Nothing truly worthwhile can be achieved without this concentration, this absence of distraction, this ability to take one's time. No one would think of dividing their work time up into forty-five-minute portions, the rhythm of our mind, of our whole being, cannot be mechanised in that way. If our activities are to bear fruit, they have to take place at their own rhythm and not according to some imposed artificial system.

Finally, alongside these reasons that are inherent in the education system, there are *social phenomena* that make practising more difficult. First and foremost is the fact that many children are *spoilt*. They are accustomed to refusing demands they find taxing, to being kept amused in an undemanding way, to being stimulated by a constant stream of novelties with ever more striking effects. Such children quickly become impatient, recalcitrant and aggressive when they have to spend some time doing something not particularly attractive which they have not chosen themselves. Very often the school cannot rely on the support of parents, since they lack understanding of the importance of calm, patient practice. Added to that is the fact that many teachers are also children of the age and had little experience during their own school-days of the fulfilment that can come from persistent practice.

There are so many difficulties — too much material to cover, too little time, the pupils' recalcitrance, one's own lack of enthusiasm — that it is hard not simply to give up.

But despite all these obstacles, we cannot abandon patient and committed practice if our teaching is to be truly successful, both in the pupil's acquisition of knowledge and of skills.

Let us look at *knowledge* first. It is acquired either by personal *experience*, by personal *insight* or by *transmission through language*. As a rule, knowledge that comes from personal experience or insight does not need to be reinforced by repetition. It is different with knowledge transmitted through language, that does need to be reinforced, both to *acquire* it and to *retain* it. There can be many forms of practice, but the key element in every case is *repetition at different and increasingly long intervals*.

If people took this simple fact seriously, namely that knowledge acquired through language can only be retained by this kind of practice, lessons would be planned completely differently from the way they are today. Once one area of a subject has been dealt with teachers mostly proceed to the next and then on to the next again. What they should be doing, however, is to keep looking back to refresh their pupils' memory of the main ideas that were presented and acquired in previous lessons or projects, or even in previous years. But they simply do not have the time, and this not-having-the-time devalues everything the pupils have worked on previously.

Connected with practice in the acquisition of knowledge is *learning by heart* - that is, repeating something word for word until it is fixed in the mind. This is completely unsuited to revision for an exam on some topic. The point of learning something off by heart is to memorise the words themselves, as is the case with singing, reciting a poem or learning a role in a play. But schools have spoilt the pleasure in poems for thousands of pupils by compelling them to learn them by heart in a way that was educationally unsuitable, by showing them up in front of the class and awarding poor marks when their memory failed them. The result is that learning by heart is hardly used at all today.

But good poems one knows by heart are a treasure for life, only pupils must enjoy learning them. The best way to achieve that is by *speaking in chorus*, which has been completely abandoned today. At in-service training courses teachers repeatedly argued that each pupil should interpret the poem in his own way and that getting them to recite in chorus was to force them into a collective corset. It is interesting that this argument is not used against singing in chorus. As far as these arguments are concerned, there is no difference between singing and reciting in chorus. Thus in Zurich, for example, there is not only a chamber choir, but a chamber *speech* choir. Alongside their aesthetic value, singing and speaking together have, like instrumental ensemble playing, an intrinsic moral value. It is about shaping a communal performance, which means keeping a balance between hearing and producing sound, between fitting in and leading, between taking responsibility and delegating responsibility — all of which is profoundly characteristic of man's existence as a thinking, feeling being. An additional advantage is that in this type of learning none of the pupils are seen as failures, weaker ones can share in the successful outcome and even stammerers forget their stammer. Success does not have to be something that happens all at once, but gradually becomes apparent as reciting in chorus is practised over a period of time.

The term 'learning by heart' is, however, inappropriate for memorising names. The classic area here is botany. When I argue for a wider knowledge of plants, I often hear the argument that it is pointless to get pupils to learn the names of plants off by heart. As if that were the point! Memorising a plant's name should mean 'knowing a plant' just as one can know a person — and one can walk past a person without noticing as easily as a plant. 'To know' someone or something is to be familiar with their essential characteristics, and that means to be able to distinguish them from others. Such knowledge is always based on precise observation. Somewhere or other Goethe says, 'We only know what we see, and we only see things we know of.' The point is not to pile up knowledge we could equally well do without, but to perceive the things around us in their distinctive individuality, thus developing a closer relationship to them, which ultimately brings a greater quality of life.

Also distinct from learning by heart is the process of '*automation*'. The alphabet is learnt off by heart, while the multiplication tables are automated. In contrast to the alphabet, multiplication tables are based on understanding, but they have to be made automatic because, as one of the fundamentals of arithmetic, they make further calculations possible and relieve us of having to go through the same basic sums again and again. This comes about through a very careful arrangement of the number concepts up to a hundred and through repeated observation of the relationships between numbers. Learning arithmetical sequences off by heart is the wrong way, but that is a special problem of the early primary years, so this is not the place to go into it in detail.

And now to the question of practice in the area of skills. Although knowledge and skill should not be sharply differentiated, *absorption* is more central to the acquisition of knowledge, while the development of ability demands *personal effort*. Beyond that, knowledge operates according to the *digital* principle: we either *have* an insight, an idea, a piece of knowledge, or we *haven't*. The area of ability, however, is governed by the *analogue* principle: the greater the effort we put into practising it, the more skilled we will become at it. All skills can be improved, perfected, in principle there is no upper limit.

That is why assessments such as: 'Learning outcome achieved, partly achieved, not achieved' are not appropriate in this area. When practising a skill, each pupil should start out from his current level of ability and push his limit up a little higher. In sport, for example, he should jump as high as is *possible for him*, run as fast *as possible*, throw the ball as far *as possible*, on the basis of his physical capability. It is pointless to compare pupils with each other; each one should work at their own limit. Whether a performance is good or bad cannot be decided on an absolute scale, but from the individual *progress* made. I get annoyed when I see a slightly built twelve-year-old girl given a poor mark because she can't jump as far or as high, or throw the ball as far as the others and consequently loses her enjoyment of the subject.

Since 'Gym' has been replaced by 'Sport', this educationally inappropriate mode of assessment seems to have become the accepted norm.

But the idea that each pupil should improve his performance according to his capabilities does not apply solely in the area of physical skills. Why should a pupil with a talent for languages be allowed to lean back in class because he gets an A in every test anyway? And why should a pupil who has no gift for numbers be humiliated by comparison with the good pupils by being given poor marks?

It is not by chance that Pestalozzi was against comparing individual pupils with the others. Anyone who believes in the acquisition of skills through individual effort knows the damage that can be done if one does not take individual capabilities into consideration. Conclusion: in every form of practice, the pupil should learn to compare himself with himself and to be guided by his own innate capabilities.

Finally a word about a widespread habit in teaching: outwitting the pupils. Practising can occasionally be felt as boring and it certainly demands effort. For this reason many teachers try to sweeten the pill. For example they turn mental arithmetic into a kind of football game and whoever calls out the answer first scores a goal for their side. Clearly teachers feel they cannot expect their pupils simply to practice and therefore believe they have to get round this by tricking them into doing something they do like doing.

I do not think much, if anything at all, of such classroom tricks. Usually the 'sweetener' comes to dominate the proceedings and the main purpose gets short shrift; also we strengthen the pupils' belief that doing sums (to stick to our example) is basically uninteresting and boring. It is better to stick to the essence of what needs to be practised and aim at real efficiency. Then the pupils will discover that practising can *of itself* be rewarding, fulfilling.

In his very readable book, *Vom Geist des Übens* (On the Spirit of Practice), Otto F. von Bollnow, the philosopher mentioned at the beginning of this chapter, points to the connection between proper practising and mystical exercises. For example, Buddhist mystics have been reported to spend hours doing nothing but rule lines freehand on blank sheets of paper. In time the lines become so regular and even that the lined sheets can hardly be distinguished from printed ones. Looked at

9 'A human being is only fully human when he is practising.'

in economic terms, such an activity is absolutely futile, but looked at as practice, as a rhythmical activity that leads one farther and farther into the depths of one's own being, it is profoundly meaningful. Happy the pupils who have the opportunity to get an inkling of the fact that it is possible by practising, by the rhythmical repetition of some activity, to reach the depths of their own being.

'The secret of my educational methods consists entirely of proceeding, without any gaps, from the completion of the first to the start of the second, and in sticking to this second one until it has been mastered as perfectly as the first.'

10 **Stone by Stone**

A good teacher is a master builder carefully erecting the edifice stone by stone. He knows that first of all you need the foundations, then the walls, last the roof. The bigger the house is to be, the stronger the foundations that are needed. In this he is observing one of Pestalozzi's key principles: the principle of building up without leaving any gaps, what we might call the principle of coherence.

And in this a teacher always bears both the children and the subject in mind. The children's faculties and the skills that derive from them should be developed in an uninterrupted sequence and in a way that is psychologically appropriate. And the subject matter is to be divided up in a way that accords with both the material and the children's psychology, then worked through step by step.

This is all so obvious that I am almost embarrassed to talk about it. I do so nevertheless since masses of pupils fail in the higher classes because they have not understood elementary steps at the lower level and have not acquired fundamental skills. Many of them can still hear the teacher saying, 'I can't wait for you, I have a whole class to teach and have to get on.'

Despite that, the rule is: only continue when the pupils have properly acquired the things they need in order to *understand later units*; only continue once they have securely mastered the simpler skills on which more complex ones are based. The principles that lead to success are: progress from the easy to the difficult, from the simple to the complex, from the concrete to the abstract, from the near to the far-off (where 'near' can also mean 'psychologically near'). That is the psychologically correct way of proceeding. This *principle of coherence* is valid for all three areas: intellectual (head), emotional/moral (heart) and practical (hand). If all the new material grows organically from the foundation of what has previously been learnt, then the teaching will be in accord with the pupils' nature.

Pestalozzi compares this to a tree: the trunk rises from the roots, the branches spread out from that and leaves, blossom and fruit develop on them. In the same way a person's education should form an integrated organism that is also open to the world outside. Each part should be joined organically to the rest. And just as a young tree is always a whole organism, not half a tree, a young person must be *complete* at every stage of his development, not just half an adult. And just as nature does not skip any stage, so there should not be any gaps in our educational development. Every new experience, every new piece of knowledge, every new skill should be organically connected to the things the child has already mastered and understood.

We can clarify Pestalozzi's demand for coherent education with insights from the psychology of thought. It is a truism that concepts form the basis of our thinking and speaking. However these concepts should not lie in our minds unordered but should be woven together in a complex network of meaning. This will reflect the possible affinities, antitheses, interdependences and logical combinations of the matter contained in the concepts. Things that belong together in any way in reality will be correspondingly linked and grouped together in our consciousness. A group of concepts which form a meaningful and coherent whole is called a *cognitive structure*. Put in modern terms then, Pestalozzi's demand for an educational process without gaps means that the teacher should be concerned to build up relevant cognitive structures in the pupils' consciousness.

The most disastrous effects of ignoring the principle of coherence can be seen in mathematics and the subjects that depend on it. Things often start to go wrong at the outset, in primary one when the concept of numbers has to be established and continues in primary two and three, when the multiplication tables have to be acquired and automated. Any child who has not mastered this foundation will fail in arithmetic at every stage. Often the teachers in the later classes, even in the final year of compulsory education, have no option but to start by securing these elementary foundations, because otherwise everything is shaky.

But 'coherence' is not required in mathematics alone, it is necessary in every subject. This is particularly difficult in history, for no historical event can be properly understood without knowledge of preceding events. That is the reason why in many schools the systematic study of history starts with prehistory — with the well-known result that pupils hardly hear anything about modern history because of lack of time. I will return to this in chapter 17.

The problem with history shows that Pestalozzi's demand for education without gaps can be fundamentally misunderstood, namely as a demand for complete knowledge in every subject. This is not only impossible, it is also undesirable. No one would have been more vehemently opposed to the pointless accumulation of knowledge than Pestalozzi. The principle of coherence, of not leaving gaps, does not concern the amount of material but the progression from one stage to the next described here. All of this requires the teacher to allow the child to *take time* at every step in his development, to learn at *leisure*. Nothing is more harmful than to attempt to achieve a lot in a short time. The result will mean knowledge and ability that are superficial and will not provide a firm foundation for what is to be learnt later. On this Pestalozzi says: *In general the methods of my approach to education do not aim at rapid success, nor do they promise it. Humans are the only creatures that Nature brings up slowly and that is what we must do as well; all of Nature's methods banish the outward show of unripe results and require us to wait and trust in long, mundane elementary exercises.*

It is impossible to follow the principle of coherence if a teacher teaches *the class*. Teaching in the spirit of Pestalozzi is always about educating *individual* pupils, even when working with the whole class. Every child has different abilities and if the teacher does not take them into account then there are bound to be gaps in the sense described above. And those children will lose their enjoyment of and interest in school work, since either too much or too little is asked of them. Thus Pestalozzi's principle is very closely connected to what we call *individualisation*.

Unfortunately the concept of 'individualisation' is used in various senses nowadays. Individualisation in the spirit of Pestalozzi does not mean each pupil has to have his own learning programme, it certainly does not mean isolation and absolutely not the possibility of shortening schooling by one or two years, depending on ability. Individualisation and regular class-teaching are not mutually exclusive. What individualisation means is taking the individuality, the unique nature, of each child seriously and fostering it; it means giving each child our full attention, knowing the way he thinks in the context of a learning sequence and what his difficulties are. Every 'wrong' answer, every awkward remark, every time he falters reflects the way the child is thinking, the way he feels. In such situations the principle of coherence becomes concrete action: the teacher finds the reason for the child's faltering or clumsiness, works out in seconds what small steps need to be taken, and in what order, so that the child can overcome the difficulty little by little. It is not sufficient to take the principle of coherence into account only when planning the year's course or a single unit, it must become second nature to the teacher so that he follows it automatically whenever a difficulty crops up.

For example: an eleven-year-old cannot pronounce the French word 'attention', even though the teacher has said it for him several times. Listening carefully, he realises that the pupil does not know which syllables have to be pronounced nasally. The teacher therefore gets him to practise each syllable separately, then the first two together, then the last two together, continuing in that way until finally all four syllables are joined and pronounced correctly. But he does not insist it must be done quickly, he lets the pupil start by saying the word slowly, then gradually speed up. (You think that is a matter of course? Not worth going into? I happen to have encountered this situation during a school visit and the teacher, who was working with a small group, allowed me to help the pupil. Practising the word lasted a good minute. You should have seen the broad smile on the boy's face when he managed something he'd always had trouble with before. The shining eyes of a child who has been successful — is that not one of the most glorious things in the world?)

As we read in the newspapers towards the end of 2006, a young man of eighteen sprayed bullets all round 'his' school in Germany before killing himself. In his farewell letter he said all that he had learnt there was how to be a failure. It makes me think back to the teacher saying, 'I can't wait for you, I have a whole class to teach.'

Naturally I can understand teachers saying that. They are trapped in a system in which *uniformity* is the overriding factor. The principle behind the system is that in a class one must always deal with the same material, make the same demands and apply the same criteria for assessment. Almost everything that is regarded as incontrovertible today makes it more or less difficult (I'm not saying impossible) to meet the needs of the individual child: putting all the children of the same age in the same class, the use of subject-specialist teachers (that a moderate use of this is justified at secondary level, I accept), timetables with their rigid division into 45-minute periods, the excessive quantity of teaching materials, the 'one-size-fits-all' requirements, the marks or other standardised assessment systems. A further difficulty is the over-large class sizes, which, it is true, are not a result of the system but of a shortage of funding. It would be good if education policy could create the conditions and prioritise the solutions which guarantee the classroom teacher the freedom that is necessary for individualised teaching.

'Of necessity the first thing I had to do was to awaken their innermost being itself and stimulate a sense of morality and justice within them in order to make them active, attentive, receptive and obedient for the world outside.'

11 **Openness!**

It sometimes happens that however well prepared a teacher is, however much effort he puts into his teaching, things just refuse to work. The pupils simply sit there in covert or undisguised protest because they are expected to make an effort. Anything is more interesting than what the teacher is trying to put over about the topic. The diagnosis: *the pupils have shut themselves off.*

It goes without saying that success in the classroom depends not only on the *teacher* but on the *pupils* as well, and the pupils' most important contribution is *openness.*

The way I see it is that our lives are played out between two opposite poles and in every situation the 'art of living' consists in combining them in a liveable synthesis. The fundamental polarity is that between productivity and receptivity: on the one hand a person must *go out of himself, actively engage with the world,* on the other he must *accept facts, be open to impressions.*

One variant of this polarity is the contrast between 'preserving one's integrity', 'warding off influences' and 'opening up', 'exposing oneself'. Both of these are necessary. Self-assertion is required when one has to win through in the 'struggle for existence' or is threatened; when, on the other hand, it is one's own psychological and intellectual growth – *education in the widest sense* – that is at stake, it is the opposite attitude that is required: engaging with things, allowing oneself to be moved, impressed, being open.

Education always involves some kind of *change* in a person. Anyone who insists on staying the way he always was is not open to education. Education is therefore always a challenge, a step into the unknown, the uncertain, and often appears threatening. A pupil's heart and mind must be prepared, must have the desire to engage with things that are new to him. First and foremost he must abandon his prejudices, refrain from jumping to conclusions. Pestalozzi himself recognised how counterproductive it is to make premature judgments on things one ought first to become acquainted with through committed learning. He was, he insisted, *not at all in favour of encouraging the children to make apparently mature, though in fact premature, judgments on any object; rather he believed in stopping them from doing that for as long as possible, until they had observed the object they were to comment on from all sides and in different conditions and were fully acquainted with the words that describe its essence and qualities.*

I would like to illustrate these thoughts with an incident from my own experience. For almost twenty years I tried, while I was involved in a special education project, to help sixteen-year-old trainee teachers develop an understanding and appreciation of classical music. My initial aim in this was to get the students to put aside their prejudices and engage with sounds which were unfamiliar to most of them but which are, after all, a significant component of Western culture. I often felt that the premature judgment and consequent dismissal of anything new, instead of listening with an open ear, open to the effect of the music, had become almost standard practice. Once I put on a CD of the aria from Bach's *Goldberg Variations*, played by Glenn Gould, in the very first lesson and asked the students to say what they thought of what they had heard. Their comments were unanimously negative: 'The pianist is obviously a beginner, it's probably a recording made after a few piano lessons.' — 'No, the playing isn't that bad, it just needs to be a bit faster and a bit louder here and there.' — 'The "song" hasn't enough class, no rhythm.' — 'The "song" ought to be played on the violin, then it wouldn't sound bad.' — 'The "song" is too long.' — 'Why is there no one singing?' — 'In a word, this composer isn't up to much.'

After these comments I couldn't resist giving them a bit of a shock. 'Is that what you think?' I said. 'That was composed by one of the greatest geniuses ever and the pianist is one of the most important musicians of this century. I don't want you to pass judgment, I want you to listen closely to what's happening and to pay attention to what's going on inside you. It's not a question of whether you like the music, but of how far we are all in a position to get something out of it and if possible understand it.' I played the piece again and, lo and behold, the students said what they had really heard and what they had felt inside themselves.

That gave me the opportunity to talk to them about the attitude of *openness* and I was pleased how quickly they came to see the demands that must be made if education is to come about. This attitude of openness could be put into words in the following way: 'I can see the danger, the obstacle to learning, if my attitude to new material is fundamentally sceptical and dismissive and I thus make judgments that are not based on understanding of the matter in question. I am therefore prepared to set aside all my prejudices and to be open to the things I have to deal with and to their effect on me. The extent to which this new material suits me and the way in which I can fit it in with everything that I already have inside me, is something that will happen automatically as I deal honestly and openly with it.'

Just as they have prejudices regarding music, most young people have similar prejudices against art, especially modern art. Many regard it as a con, merely a way of making money. Here too, as with every other topic they are confronted with at school, we must start by getting the pupils to adopt an attitude of openness. Only then will they be prepared to see a picture in its own terms, as a picture and nothing else, to look at it objectively, to allow it to speak to them. Thus my pupils learnt to appreciate the fundamental difference between the question, 'What's that supposed to be?' and the question, 'What is that?' Anyone asking the first question is already convinced it's a load of rubbish; anyone asking the second is open and ready to accept an answer.

For us teachers that naturally leads to the question of how we can produce this open, receptive attitude, the readiness to learn and change, in our pupils. For that we need something that helps a pupil to open up, without which it is even impossible for some — *genuine authority*. Had I not sensed, in the class with the trainee teachers, that I was accepted by them and that therefore what I said counted for something, I would certainly have refrained from my 'shock tactics'. To engage with something new is always a challenge, and the trust created by genuine authority encourages pupils to accept the challenge. And the pupils' trust in their teacher will allow him — at least in the higher years — to keep bringing up the question of openness and thus make it clear that he expects them to open up to new topics.

We can only achieve openness as a general basic attitude on the part of the pupils if we take constant care to ensure that the pupils *can* open up. That is only possible if the atmosphere in the class is calm. If one bombards them with information and tasks, this atmosphere will be destroyed and the pupils will go on the defensive. Openness can only be created and maintained when we give every word its due weight and give the pupils time to understand its meaning and to allow it to have effect. It is also important that the pupils be able to sense that the teacher himself is engaged with what he is saying. If we are not ourselves involved with the food for the mind we present to our pupils, it will leave them cold as well.

The teacher's authority automatically brings to mind the converse on the part of the pupils: *obedience* and *discipline*. Only pupils who are obedient and disciplined are capable of learning. But since it has become difficult to talk about obedience and discipline nowadays, I will treat them in more detail in separate chapters. It will turn out that the openness I demand here is, in a certain respect, identical to obedience and discipline.

'A child's obedience and acceptance of its natural status do not follow on from the completion of education, they must be the basic foundation of education from the very beginning.'

12 **Obedience — No thanks!**

The Nazis have given obedience a bad name. They got people to believe obedience was a virtue *in itself*. But since then people have come to realise that obedience can only serve life if it is combined with *insight* and genuine *freedom*.

I still cannot understand why I regularly met with discontent and rejection, even aggressiveness, at the mere mention of the word 'obedience'. In practical terms the plain and simple truth is that all of our activity as teachers rests on our pupils' willingness to obey. I would like to examine this contradiction by demonstrating the general importance of obedience within the context of our existence as human beings.

Let us start with the psychology of perception. As is well known, we human beings have the ability *not* to see the world as a chaos of unconnected stimuli; instead in the act of perception we assign a *meaning* to everything that comes into contact with our senses. In a sense we, as perceiving subjects, *create* the world we experience as we interpret the stimuli.

A key element of this way of processing stimuli by interpreting them is that we do *not* perceive the 'objects' of our field of perception as isolated facts but as things that belong together in some way that makes sense. Perception creates a *structure* of meanings. This is generally referred to as a *situation*. There is almost no point in giving examples, for ultimately every existential act which can be expressed in language takes place within a structure of meaning that can be termed a 'situation'. We are waiting outside an occupied telephone kiosk, we are working in the garden, we are involved in a road accident, we go to an exhibition, we stand looking at a picture. The last two examples show that transferring our attention to a smaller or larger area simultaneously redefines the situation which forms the background to our experience.

These fundamental considerations have a logical connection with the nature of obedience. As active subjects, we experience the situation obtaining at any moment not as something neutral but as a state of affairs that *makes demands on us*. The extent to which these demands are an acquired response is unimportant in this connection. All that interests us here is to establish that in any situation we find ourselves in we naturally feel ourselves exposed to the demand that we observe the rules of behaviour that are inseparable from the nature of the situation. Thus the quiet atmosphere of a church demands silence, or at least that we speak softly, are dressed appropriately and make gentle movements. But the demands inherent in a discotheque, on a beach, at an office desk, on a path through the woods, in a kitchen shortly after a meal or a at vertical cliff-face are quite different. Our lives as individuals as well as our social lives are largely activated and controlled by the fact that we quite naturally submit to the demands made by the situation of the moment. In other words, it is the most natural thing in the world for us to behave in a manner appropriate to the situation. Or to put it another way, we obey the demand that is part of our perception of a given situation.

Thus a 'situation' becomes an *authority* which we obey in the overwhelming majority of cases and *obedience*, understood as behaving in line with an authority, which by no means has to be a person, is almost as much a matter of course for an adult as eating and breathing. *Inappropriate behaviour* therefore, is almost the equivalent of *existential disobedience*. People are disobedient in this sense, then, if they fool around on dangerous, steep terrain, run out into a busy street without paying attention to the traffic, leave dangerous chemicals within reach of children, dump rubbish in the woods or disturb the devotions of people praying in church by laughing and joking.

The question naturally arises as to why we are prepared to obey without giving it a second thought. There are presumably two main reasons: in the first place, we often project the rules into the situation ourselves, with the result that they agree with our own values and we consequently feel it is good and sensible to observe them. In the second place, ignoring the rules appropriate to a situation often incurs unpleasant consequences: we can have an accident, be an embarrassment, fail, be rejected, criticised, perhaps even fined or punished, all of which create disagreeable feelings.

As well as these psychological reasons for our everyday obedience, however, we must also consider its essential *meaning*. Communication and social behaviour are very largely dependent on countless situations being perceived by different people in a more or less identical manner. If that were not the case, we would each of us be living in a world of our own. It is only the fact that most people quite automatically behave in a way that is appropriate to the situation that makes our social life bearable. If they didn't, our world would be like a madhouse, and that would make individuals even more insane than they already are. Or to put it in less drastic terms: the fact that most people unquestioningly behave in the manner demanded by the situation guarantees that we can assume as given the minimal conditions that are indispensable if we are to shape our own positive lifestyle.

That does not of course touch on the question of whether, and to what extent, observing such rules of behaviour in particular cases is also *morally good*. There are many situations where the behaviour which seems appropriate is, from a higher point of view, reprehensible. We only need to observe the behaviour of individuals when their club has lost a match, when a large number of the group are drunk or have taken drugs, when a fight is going on in the street or when a horde of soldiers goes from village to village, burning, murdering, and raping. Then things are done which even those who do them cannot understand once they are away from the destructive situation. Given this, young people should be brought up to observe the rules when they have a positive effect and do not contravene morality, but to refuse to obey the prevailing rules when what the situation suggests would involve them in destructive and morally reprehensible behaviour.

This brings us to upbringing and obedience both at home and in school. Since young people need to learn to behave in an appropriate manner, those responsible for their upbringing have to demand obedience. They do not do so simply to satisfy their lust for power. On the contrary, it is tedious when one is compelled to exercise power and require obedience, but one does so despite that so that pupils will learn to recognise the rules inherent in a situation and follow them — insofar as they are morally acceptable. Thus authority that demands obedience always appears as the *guardian of a situation that regulates life*. Thus a teacher will take action if, in an arithmetic class, one of the pupils folds the exercise sheet into a paper aeroplane and sends it flying over the heads of his classmates, who are at work; the same behaviour could be acceptable in the next class, handicraft, it all depends on the situation.

If I were in charge of a class today, I would talk to my pupils about what I have said here again and again. I would show them how every adult responds to the demands of situations with automatic obedience morning, noon and night. I would show them that having to obey is not something that stops once we are grown up; on the contrary, being able to obey is part of the make-up of a responsible adult and that behaving in conformity with the situation is a sign of true maturity.

Beyond that, I would also show them that one must be able to refuse to behave as a situation suggests, be rebellious or even revolutionary. I would also make it clear that one must not mistake obstinate defiance, insistence on selfish interests for a refusal that comes from one's conscience, from a genuine sense of responsibility. And I would never dream of inciting my pupils to revolt against all adaptation to social conventions or of encouraging them to confuse immature rebelliousness with true independence.

Apart from this general objective of developing in young people a true sense of obedience and the ability to act on it, we must ask ourselves what its significance is for improving the quality of education. The answer is clear: it is an essential *precondition* for education. The foundations and goals of school as an institution (compulsory education, timetable, syllabus) assume the obedience of pupils, parents and teachers as a matter of course. Without obedience it is impossible to organise teaching. That is such a matter of course that nothing further need be said.

Of much greater significance is obedience as a psychological foundation allowing education in the true sense of the word — the shaping, development and extension of a pupil's personality — to take place.

Obedience is the readiness to respond positively to objective demands and precisely that is necessary to learn anything at all. That is why *wilfulness* is — along with lack of ability — one of the main obstacles to achieving the desired result in education. Unfortunately, a pupil's wilfulness is often misinterpreted as showing that he has a mind of his own, is capable of independent thought. These are naturally desirable virtues and to be encouraged; in contrast to them, wilfulness has no objective foundation and is always destructive. Wilfulness is always — against all logic and all objective demands — a matter of refusal or at best of doing things differently, of being different on principle, of self-assertion as a disastrous form of compensation. If a teacher fails to recognise wilfulness in a pupil and — with much patience and understanding — gradually overcome it, it will turn into stubbornness and ultimately into a complete refusal to cooperate. Such people are incapable of seeing anything objectively — the precise opposite of what was discussed in the previous chapter as an essential condition for education: openness.

To sum up: the ability to obey is not just an educational target to make social life possible, nor just a necessary condition for the organisation of teaching. Beyond that it is the fundamental attitude of being prepared to accept things, to engage with new things, and is thus a basis for learning, for education and, especially, for the improvement of the quality of education. In contrast, a refusal to accept anything new or different, wilfulness and obstinacy are fundamental obstacles to learning, to education, which need to be recognised in the early stages and handled with psychologically based educational strategies.

It is not only today that obedience has become a problem of educational theory, it was for Pestalozzi too. As a student of Rousseau, he tried to bring up his own son without requiring obedience. As his diary fragment of 1774 shows, he very quickly abandoned this. Like a conscientious bookkeeper, he weighed the arguments for freedom and for obedience against each other and came to the following significant conclusion: *Truth is not one-sided. Freedom is a blessing and so is obedience. We must join together what Rousseau separated. Convinced that an unwise restriction demeaning mankind was a cause of misery, he set no limit to freedom.*

A good twenty-five years later, asking himself which psychological faculties of the infant were to be fostered in order to develop its moral life, Pestalozzi came up with the three basic moral emotions: love, trust and gratitude. And he recognised obedience as the indispensable foundation of moral behaviour. He believed that anyone who believes they can do without that abandons the child to a life of indiscipline.

'The silence I insisted on when I was there and teaching was a great means to achieving my goal.'

13 Discipline Means: Being There

A few years ago there was a late-night discussion on Swiss television about school uniforms and discipline. Uniforms and discipline? Are we in the army? I do not propose to argue about whether we need uniforms in school or not, but education is unthinkable without discipline. Why?

As human beings we are constantly prey to sense impressions or physical urges. And there are always things going on inside our heads as well. All kinds of thoughts, imaginings, memories, ideas and visions of the future jostle for our attention. The more responsive a person is, the more receptive to impulses from within and stimuli from outside, the more they are in danger of dissipating their energies.

To counter this, each one of us possesses the power of *concentration*. We are able to ignore the variety that presents itself to us at any one moment and devote ourselves to one single issue. By so doing we achieve depth and a solid foundation, both in the matter in question and inside ourselves.

Concentration and dissipation are not, however, two poles of equal value, such as activity and passivity. It is certainly not a case where we should 'choose the happy medium' and not let ourselves get entirely bound up in concentration, but enjoy the seductive attractions of variety as well. This, I admit, is a fundamental ethical decision. I agree with Angelus Silesius: 'Man, find your essence.' One could also say, 'Man, find yourself.' This is our main task in life and allowing ourselves to be pulled this way and that is a latent danger. Only the practice of concentration can take us closer to our goal, for that alone gives us conscious and deliberate commitment. Squandering our energies on everything from inside or outside that attracts our attention and is not subject to conscious evaluation, takes place without the involvement of our will. It simply happens to us. But if we consciously resist it, then we are no longer *being lived* by various kinds of stimuli, we ourselves *are living* in the true sense of the word.

Everything mankind has ever thought up or created rests on this ability to curb the centrifugal forces within us by concentrating on one single thing at a time. This is also true of what Pestalozzi calls the 'creation of one's self' which every one of us has to work at. And we can only do that by concentrating on the tasks that prove necessary for this process of education in the widest sense.

One might object that a person who, after a few seconds, turns his attention from one thing to another and then to another is concentrating during those seconds. But taking notice in this way is not the result of a conscious effort and as a rule does not contribute to education. What is required is the ability to concentrate on a single matter over a lengthy period, and this ability is called 'discipline'. I repeat: education without discipline is impossible.

The key question of course is: how do we get the pupils to behave in a disciplined manner and thus to concentrate on their school work? There are no simple answers but it is an important step if the teacher is convinced that discipline is not simply something he *can* demand but something he *must* demand and establish himself. And the first commandment is: when teaching, always keep your eye on all the pupils. Make sure they look at you when you are speaking. Do not continue speaking if pupils are talking among themselves or not paying attention. What you say is always important or you wouldn't say it.

Part of the art of teaching is the ability to bring pupils' attention back to the matter in hand or to react to conversations among them in a way that does not disturb the class's concentration even more. Politeness, gentle humour, a smile, a look, half a step in the direction of those talking, are more effective than coming down hard and making a show of the miscreants. It would, though, be unrealistic to expect to achieve discipline without having occasionally to exercise one's authority, or even one's power. A reprimand will not guarantee that the pupil will really concentrate on his work, but it will reduce the possibility of him distracting others, even the whole class.

However, it is just as unrealistic to think that the discipline needed for education can be basically or, indeed, solely achieved by pressure in an atmosphere of fear. True discipline only comes about when work on a task gives pleasure and is felt to be rewarding. And that can only happen with teaching that takes account of the age and the individual needs of the pupils and is thus in accord with their human nature, as Pestalozzi recommended. This brings me back, as so often, to the point where I must say that none of my suggestions can be realised in isolation. Everything supports everything else. Teaching that is in accord with human nature is a world, a living organism.

'Observation of Nature itself is the true foundation of human instruction because it is the sole foundation of human knowledge.'

Consign Paper to the
14 **Rubbish Bin**

Have you, as a parent or teacher, had a look in your child's schoolbag recently? If so, I hope you are one of the fortunate ones who can say, 'I didn't find any crumpled-up worksheets that were completed months ago, nor any A4 sheets on which just a few lines had been written before they too were stuffed in the schoolbag. And I'm glad to say I didn't find any 'weighty' books, which, although scarcely used at all, had to be carried to school and home again day after day. And the worksheet folder had the full set of sheets, all carefully completed and arranged according to topic.'

Or have you looked at your office or your desk or even, if you like, your bookshelves and wished all paper were consigned to the waste bin? Did the devil perhaps create not just paper money, as we hear in Goethe's *Faust II*, but paper in general?

Let us get back to Pestalozzi. He did use a lot of paper himself — the critical edition of his writings runs to forty-five volumes — but he tended to feel that paper was unsuitable as a basis for acquiring knowledge. So the first thing he did when, at the age of forty-five, he was given the chance to try out his educational ideas in a corner of the schoolroom of Dysli, the shoemaker, was to put away all the pious books. It created a scandal. Instead, he got the pupils to stroke the dilapidated walls with their fingers and say things such as, 'The wallpaper is rough. Here is a hole in the wall.'

Pestalozzi opposed the manner of teaching that was current at the time in which pupils spent years laboriously learning to read from books they did not understand and talking about things of which they had no personal experience and could not really comprehend. Pestalozzi battled untiringly against this use of empty words, this 'idle prating', this 'chitter-chatter' as he called it. What was clear to him was that before one can *read* one must be able to *speak*, and one can only speak when one is *thinking* what one is saying. But thinking rests on clear *concepts* and these, in turn, rest on the real *observation* of things. Thus Pestalozzi arrived at his thesis '*that observation is the absolute foundation of all knowledge.*'

A teacher who wants to develop his pupils' faculties of mind in a natural way must therefore make sure that they perceive real things *with all their senses* — by seeing, hearing, touching, smelling and tasting. In so doing he is using *observation* as the basis on which he can build up all further reflection on and discussion of objects about which he is teaching them.

Pestalozzi makes a theoretical distinction between *four stages of observing the outside world*:

In the first stage, that of *dark* observation, simple stimuli are recorded by our sense organs, as happens with animals as well. Pestalozzi therefore often calls this mode of perception 'animal observation'.

But the second stage, like the further stages, is only possible for humans, for in it we become aware of precise form, are clear about number and can use language to name an object or objects. Pestalozzi calls this stage of observation *definite* observation.

In the third stage of observation as many of our sense organs as possible should be employed to determine the further characteristics, for example the texture of the surface, the colour, temperature, sound, taste, smell, weight, consistency. That turns definite observation into *clear* observation, which must always be accompanied by naming the characteristics. Thus at this stage the pupils can not only name the object itself but also find the appropriate expressions for its characteristics. That, however, is only possible if the senses have been intensively trained. The training of the senses, the observation of concrete objects and the linguistic processing must always go hand in hand with each other.

In the fourth stage the object is shown in various relationships which are not immediately accessible to the senses. It is only exceptionally that pupils can discover them from their own investigations, as a rule they have to be taught them. Thus for example they will learn what an object is used for, who produced it, how it has developed in the course of history, with what other objects it is closely related, what its value is, what hidden dangers it has. As the pupils acquire this knowledge, clear observation becomes a *distinct concept*. Knowledge about an object can, of course, be extended indefinitely, so a distinct concept is not something final but can be broadened and deepened in the course of one's life.

In practice these four stages cannot be separated in the classroom, but it is helpful if a teacher remains aware of the essentials: starting out from real objects, involving all the senses, formulating observations precisely, differentiating between the acquired concepts through the teachers' explanations.

The acquisition of distinct concepts is the basis for two of the most important human faculties, which are intimately related: *thought* and *speech*. But that is not the end of a pupil's intellectual development for in a mature person fully developed thought expresses itself in correct *judgment*. If thought is based on real *observation,* then the judgments that are based on it will derive from a true understanding of the facts and not be a simple regurgitation of the undigested opinions of other people. In other words, education based on observation will guide young people to *truth. Living in truth is the ultimate goal of intellectual development.*

Naturally this requires time. *Passing judgment* is not a matter for small children, it is an ability that matures slowly. Pestalozzi is quite clear about this: *I believe the time for learning is not the time for making judgments; the time for making judgments starts with the completion of learning, with the ripening of the causes for which one makes judgments, has the right to make judgments; and I believe that every judgment should have inner truth for the individual who delivers it, should emerge from a comprehensive knowledge of these causes as mature and complete as a ripened seed falls, freely and without the use of force, out of the husk.*

In our modern schools, however, pupils mostly get their knowledge second hand, they memorise what others have discovered. Naturally that is understandable and justified over large areas of the curriculum. It only becomes problematical if it makes it as good as impossible for pupils to make their own observations and acquire knowledge independently, and if even in those areas where that would be possible, they are allowed to take the easier, though less educationally valuable route of acquiring knowledge ready-made. On the general level of the organisation of education, this appears in an unfortunate dominance of paper and electronic media.

From Pestalozzi's point of view we must oppose this trend with the battle cry: Back to the phenomena! But a teacher can only take this demand seriously insofar as he has the freedom to turn to those phenomena that are in the immediate vicinity of the school. And he can only do that if he is not compelled to feed his pupils standardised Euro-fare that has been pre-packaged in units with the associated teaching materials.

Pestalozzi's reasons for using materials from the immediate vicinity as a starting point are not purely educational. He felt it was important that people should be firmly rooted in the concrete situations in which they had to conduct their lives. Anyone who at first finds his everyday surroundings problematic, but then faces up to them by observing and thinking, will build up vital forces within himself, which will encourage him to act responsibly within his environment.

Mastery of the craft of teaching reveals itself in the proper treatment of phenomena in the classroom. Such a teacher will know what skills he can develop in the pupils through dealing directly with phenomena, what important basic concepts he can impart and what practical advantages for teaching he can exploit:

- In general it is easier to arouse pupils' enthusiasm for working on an object or theme from real life than for studying prescribed texts and images. It can turn a lesson into an experience, removing the sense of artificiality. The pupils hardly see it as 'learning' at all. They feel the way we adults do when we go to a foreign country. In general we do not go there with the purpose of acquiring knowledge but for the experience; with that, however, the extension of our knowledge comes automatically. Knowledge is not the *purpose* but the *result* of the undertaking. Knowledge as a waste product, if you like, what is left over after we have occupied ourselves heart, soul and senses with some phenomenon.

- As regards its treatment in class, a real phenomenon is always *more open* than any kind of presentation on paper or screen. This openness makes it possible to contemplate different objectives or to bring them into the lesson spontaneously. That makes the pupils' contribution more important. In particular, however, the teacher can develop the pupils' sense of how to go about discovering things for themselves when confronted with some phenomenon. In this way the pupils learn the basic techniques of research and develop curiosity and genuine interests.

- An important aspect of this exploration of phenomena is the employment of all the relevant *senses*. Thus direct contact with phenomena helps to train the senses and develop the habit of using them. This can only happen through hands-on experience, through direct observation of a phenomenon.

- The fact that the pure phenomenon, which has not been specially prepared for teaching purposes, is open in all directions, makes it particularly suitable and fruitful in helping pupils *learn to ask illuminating questions.* They should discover that education does not just mean giving the right answers; that putting the right questions is at least as important.

- *Observation* is only fully developed when sense perception and questioning combine. By learning to observe correctly, pupils acquire an important basis for coping with problems, but also a means of enriching their inner life.

- Asking the right kind of questions, using all one's senses, observing precisely and thinking logically ultimately lead to new knowledge which the pupil — together with the teacher and the rest of the class — *has acquired himself.* Knowledge acquired in this way is unlikely to be forgotten.

- Finally, the pupils learn to express their new knowledge *in language* and to present it in a pleasing and proper form in text and pictorial representations they have made themselves.

This last point brings us to one of Pestalozzi's important principles: namely that the teaching of factual subjects (science, local history) and of the mother tongue should always go together. In concrete terms this means that the teacher and pupils will spend enough time examining a phenomenon thoroughly for the pupils to be clear in their minds about it and able to write a description in their own words. This is much more productive than doing a final test with a series of separate questions. Pupils who know from experience that they are expected to report on any topic fully and in their own words will approach a new area of knowledge with that in mind right from the start. And the teacher does not have to depend on the answers to tests for assessment, but can get a much more precise idea of how well a particular pupil has mastered the material.

Naturally this all requires sufficient time. Since, however, schools nowadays are so organised down to the last detail that they feel this time is not available, they attempt to save time by using 'more efficient methods'. The solution appears to lie in something that has established an almost tyrannical hold over educational practice today: the so-called *worksheet*. It contains brief information, questions to be answered, perhaps pictures or small tasks to be carried out. On pre-printed lines or in gaps in the text pupils have to insert specialist terms, answer questions, perhaps even formulate a discovery in a short sentence. The perceived advantages of using such worksheets are that the pupils will be active during the lesson, at the same time committing the results to memory as a basis for revision and the following achievement test, and that in comparison with the process described above time will be saved.

In principle it is necessary to use the time available efficiently, but this must not be an absolute requirement. A completely rationalised learning process makes it difficult to take account of the particular class, of individual pupils and the specific learning situation; it also makes it difficult to pursue the topic into areas that are not allowed for in the plan. Moreover it is not necessarily a good idea to try and *make things easier* for the pupils with printed handouts since a pupil's *exer-*

tion is identical with 'the use of faculties' and thus with *the fundamental requirement for the development of faculties.* In this respect the habitual use of printed worksheets is questionable. Pupils save time and energy, but that means that lower demands are made on their powers, which in turn means a loss of education. For this reason I believe that the best work sheet is a blank piece of paper.

The demand, central to both educational theory and practice, that teachers and pupils should devote their attention as far as possible to the phenomenon itself does not fit in well with the standard 45-minute period. This dominates the whole of teaching, especially at senior secondary level. At worst this system can mean that pupils have to deal with up to ten subject areas in any one day - a psychological impossibility. A change to the system is urgently needed here.

The solution is relatively simple: the *four-phase timetable.* After deducting weeks devoted to sport, special topics and projects, the remaining school time is divided into four phases (A, B, C, D) of equal length. Half of the subjects are taught in phases A and C, the other half in phases B and D, but with twice as many hours per week as at present. That in principle means the end of the stand-alone 45-minute lesson. Two timetables are drawn up for the whole of the school year. The two subjects that remain outside this arrangement are sport and instrumental tuition, which are taught throughout the year. Depending on the local situation and questions of personnel, other subjects can be accommodated in the timetable in the traditional way.

The four-phase timetable favours 'epoch teaching' (as practised for example in the Waldorf schools), makes it possible to linger over a topic and is the best way of organising teaching to take account of all the concerns expressed in this book. It has the advantage of having been tried out: at the teacher training college where I worked it was used successfully over many years. Doubling the weekly periods per subject made projects possible which could hardly be undertaken with the normal timetable: student plays in German or a foreign language, geological or botanical outings, historical research 'on site', attendance at outside events, practical experiments in chemistry, biology and physics, choir projects.

Essential for the realisation of the four-phase timetable, however, are the good will and flexibility of all concerned. It is occasionally unavoidable that a teacher will have to take two periods more than the norm in one phase and two periods less in the other. The more closely knit a school community, the easier it is to organise a four-phase timetable. And anyway, concentrating pupils in large campuses is educationally counterproductive.

'Life forms us and the life that forms us is not a matter of words, but of deeds.'

15 **Great — All Those Holidays!**

Why do teachers have such long holidays? Because of the pupils, of course. But why do the pupils have such long holidays? No, not because our forefathers were particularly fond of children, nor so that we can go to the seaside in the summer. When primary education became general, European society was still largely agrarian, so children were freed from school when they were needed on the farm: in spring to clear the meadows and plough the fields, in summer for haymaking, in late summer for the grain harvest, in autumn to harvest fruit and root vegetables. Thus there were no holidays in winter, just a few days round Christmas, no question of skiing holidays. When I started teaching in a small rural community in Switzerland in 1954, I didn't have a single, long summer holiday, but two weeks each during haymaking and the harvest. These were announced at short notice, depending on the weather, by the chairman of the local school board.

So now we have our thirteen weeks' holiday whether we like it or not, even though the pupils are not needed to work on the farms any more. We are quite justifiably envied our holidays, for they are a marvellous opportunity (which would be welcomed by members of other professions as well). We can recuperate from the stressful work, prepare for the next session and pursue our own interests.

Interests? Hobbies? During holidays paid for by the state! Some people don't like the sound of that, but they're wrong, for the children get the benefit.

There is no other profession where one's private life has such a direct and obvious effect on one's work, which does not just consist of giving lessons using prepared material. If it did, the teaching would be dead. As a teacher one must mean something to the pupils, must be a model, a person they can talk to, a person who inspires them, and one can do that better the broader one's horizon, the deeper one goes into areas one is interested in. For that reason it is bad for the pupils if young teachers only remain in the profession for a few years. The older one is and the more intensively one has lived, the more things one has learnt, practised and studied, the greater the wealth of experience one can draw on. A teacher who enjoys teaching knows that his whole life, all his activities, everything he does, everything he reads, collects and creates is ultimately genuine preparation for his teaching. It is the foundation for specific preparation related to particular subjects or lessons.

The sum of available knowledge is unlimited. Compared with it, the little one can impart at school is not even a drop in the ocean. I do not see why this little knowledge has to be the same for all pupils. Only a small part of the knowledge contained in our syllabuses is necessary for their future lives. That can be standardised. Beyond that, however, *what* they learn is almost irrelevant. The decisive factor is *how* they learn and whether their *faculties and aptitudes* are *developed* as well as possible.

It can only be desirable, then, that every teacher should use his own interests, which he does really know about, as a topic for lessons. A beekeeper will talk about bees in great detail in biology; an amateur astronomer will be able to relate many aspects of science to his own specialism; a plant collector will spend more time on botany than a herpetologist; and anyone who paints, or writes, or composes songs will also exploit that in his teaching.

Of course, not all hobbies are equally suitable for use in school. I have nothing against, say, wine buffs, but a local historian would find his interest much more useful from a professional point of view. There is a very wide range of interests and activities one can pursue with some passion but there are some that are very central to our cultural and social existence as human beings. In my opinion these are philosophy (including theology) and psychology, history, politics and art, in the latter especially literature, fine art and music. Anyone who has no interest at all in these areas should not become a teacher.

There are two reasons why I consider an *interest in art* indispensable for a teacher:

In the first place anyone who occupies himself with art develops and refines his own *sensibility*, that is, his perception and judgment in matters of the mind and spirit. Sensibility is a measure of the development of mind and spirit. As teachers it is our task to assist the pupils in their own development and we can only do this to the extent that we have developed ourselves. No one can give more than they have.

In the second place, anyone who occupies himself seriously with the arts will encounter a wealth and an immense variety of expressions of the *human spirit* and this is one of the most enriching experiences open to us. The pupils of a teacher who knows something about the arts, who loves and values paintings, books and music, can hardly avoid profiting from this richness of spirit.

Acquiring expertise in art requires academic study and that is not what we are talking about here. What we are talking about is living with works of art, allowing them to enrich our lives, developing our judgment so that we can distinguish what has real quality from the superficial, from sham — that is, to acquire an understanding of art, an interest in, a love of art — for example readers who are moved by books while retaining their critical faculties, people who buy paintings, go to concerts, theatres, exhibitions. It also includes those who enjoy painting and drawing or regularly practise on a musical instrument without wanting to perform in public. A committed teacher will be glad to belong to this group, it will certainly refine his sense of quality and in many subjects this will have an effect on his choice of material and level of expectation.

This unity of a teacher's private and professional life is largely the basis for the most important psychological state for any working person: enjoyment. We teachers must do everything we can to enable us to enjoy our work. That is not only good for us — otherwise we would soon be burnt-out and fall sick — it is also good for the pupils, for anyone who enjoys his work radiates enjoyment and infects others with his enjoyment. There can be nothing better for a child than to have such a teacher at school.

Creating enjoyment is connected with other gifts every person possesses: *imagination* and *creativity*. The more a teacher can develop these two abilities and integrate them into his professional activities, the happier he will be with his work.

Imaginative and creative teachers get frustrated with prepared materials that are all-too perfect and restricting: teaching-aid systems, worksheet packages, standardised assessment units. As they become more experienced, they assume the right to include more and more of their own material in lessons. It may be convenient to copy language exercises on some topic out of a book, but it is considerably more satisfying to create an exercise of one's own for one's own pupils. And it can be tailored to their needs, taking account of their level of understanding and using material from a topic that is being dealt with at the moment in science.

And why should we not sometimes use texts of our own in reading lessons — stories, childhood memories, descriptions of journeys? If the pupils see their teacher as someone who enjoys writing, he is already halfway there in essay writing lessons (or whatever they're called). The possibilities offered by computers and word processing make this kind of thing much, much easier.

And how about a little school play? It is a pleasure to devise scenes and dialogues, and one can even write them to suit the pupils who are to play them. Everyone has the right to be a beginner; you gather experience and improve gradually. You don't have to be a Shakespeare.

And you don't have to be a Schubert when it comes to composing a song. There's no reason why you shouldn't try to compose a song yourself — perhaps with the words as well — and get the class to sing it. But you don't have to insist on only using your own creations in class.

There is plenty of scope for our creative urge in handicraft as well, in drawing, in gym, in the decoration of the classroom and, last but not least, in the organisation of each lesson. The more we manage to make use of our own creativity in the classroom, the closer we will come to the ideal: taking pleasure in our work as teachers.

Now it is possible to read all this and find some of it good but still to keep failing. Ultimately success does not solely depend on knowing a lot and having many skills and good ideas, even ideals; just as important is finding the *strength to persevere*. Knowing and using one's sources of strength is a matter of survival.

Anyone who deals with this topic must look at his own way of life as well and ask himself, 'How do I handle my own psyche?' This is very personal, so there won't be any more universally applicable answers. Each person must find their own way, but I will allow myself to make a few hints and suggestions.

In this, as in education in general, there are counteractive and supportive measures; on the one hand one must avoid things that *sap one's strength,* on the other one must find *possible sources of strength.*

One of the most strength-sapping features of modern life is rush. Everyone's in a hurry, speed is the first priority. Only someone who can do two or three things at once can keep up. Another is noise: music, music, music to drown out the traffic, the machines and anything quiet. Consumption can be strength-sapping too as can any kind of addiction. Perhaps people today are less characterised by what they do than by what they do not do.

On the other hand the first source of strength is quiet. Much comes from it: knowledge of one's self, the courage to make decisions, the impetus to act. Quiet can still, fortunately, be found: out in the countryside, in the woods, far from the crowds, in one's own home, in a church. Quiet can be cultivated by meditation. In religious people that leads to prayer.

The sister of quiet is leisure — leisure to devote oneself to one's own interests. Anyone who follows their own interests, gains strength, and anyone who finds the essence in pursuing their own interests will bear fruit. Art is mankind's attempt to find the essence and give expression to it.

And beyond all that: strength is nullified by argument and released by closeness to others. One cannot aim to be strong without seeking peace with one's fellow men.

Come back from your holidays rested and refreshed.

'During lessons you must
not burden the pupils' weak,
childish nature with your own
inadequacies. You must feed their
childish nature, which is hungry
for development.'

16 **The Moon is as Big as a Football**

'Whaat? Is that a wolf?' a disappointed primary-one boy asked his teacher during a visit to the zoo. They had had the fairy tale of Little Red Riding Hood in class, so it had seemed a good idea to have a look at a real live wolf, in line with Pestalozzi's principle of observation.

The teacher is to be congratulated. Despite that, the boy's disappointment gives one pause for thought. The wolf in the fairy tale is a myth, an image of the mind. Children sense intuitively that it belongs to a different reality, so hardly any of them wonder how an animal of that size can swallow the grandmother and then her granddaughter without injuring them, so that the hunter can release them unharmed. What Red Riding Hood complains about is not the corrosive gastric juices, disturbing intestinal rumblings and the danger of suffocation, but the darkness in the wolf's belly. There is hidden knowledge in the mind of a child of that age: all this is happening in another world, the world of dreams, of imagination, of fairy tale. And everything in a fairy tale is a symbol.

In their inner life children in kindergarten and the infants' class are still very much at home in this mythical outlook. They can effortlessly transform themselves into different beings and can reassign any object according to their immediate needs: they are a goat or a cat or even a car and the chair is a house, a piece of paper a tablecloth. And it is wonderful to be Harry Potter: you can do magic, everything is full of mysterious, living forces, nothing is dead, everything interacts with everything else. One can talk to every object, for how could it not hear, not understand anything? Children love this magical-mythical world,

111

these mysterious worlds inhabited by gnomes, elves, fairies and other fantastic beings.

Happy the child for whom this is not spoilt by a know-all adult world. In his world of the imagination he can gather fundamental psychological experience going far beyond what is possible in his real, everyday life. Thus Little Red Riding Hood, for example, can represent man as such who is given the task of helping to cure the Grandmother (whatever one understands by that) who has fallen ill. To do that, she must follow a prescribed path through life and the temptations of evil are part of it. Quite independently of theological theories, the child experiences, in the symbols of the story, the fall of man into darkness and the possibility of salvation.

As teachers we should not only *know about* the special nature of the child's world of the imagination, we should also *respect* it. A child should be allowed to live out each of his phases of development. The history of educational theory shows clearly enough that this requirement has frequently been ignored. Children were seen simply as little adults: their spontaneity and natural urges (urge to be active, play instinct, need to communicate, infantile sexual behaviour) were suppressed by authoritarian systems, which influenced everything right down to the classroom furniture, or they were manipulated and burdened with social and political problems and attitudes which they were in no position to deal with properly.

Today we imagine we have left all that behind us, and take full account of children's special nature. But I see an anti-child tendency even in our schools today. It comes out in the way *children are expected to adopt adult ways of thinking at too early a stage.*

An educated adult thinks in a way that is *rational,* that is *enlightened* and *scientific.* He accepts what can be *proved.* With phenomena he automatically looks for the *causes* and the *laws* behind them. He *abstracts* from the *concrete,* he puts everything into the coherent containers (or ones that have been forced into coherence) of his systems and regards a matter as understood when he has explained its causes and fitted it into his system.

I have nothing against that, but I think it is inappropriate to make this way of thinking the basis of the education of young children. But that is exactly what we do when, in our education courses, we do not start out from the *phenomena* as children experience them, but from *abstract scientific systems*, which are then given some 'child-friendly' coating to make them palatable for the pupils.

That applies not only to 'content' lessons, but to the teaching of the mother tongue as well. In this the living phenomenon is the language itself in all forms of usage, but not linguistic theory. From the point of view of the children's psychology it is appropriate to start by allowing language to be what it is for the child, primarily a *means of expression* and a *medium for transmitting information*. Thus initially language teaching should centre on the children's own speaking and hearing, then expose them to poems and stories — which will also enrich them mentally and emotionally; they should also learn how to read poems and stories aloud correctly and be encouraged to write their own. Depending on age, they should also practise expressions that we know cause difficulty and expand their vocabulary, starting out from the observation of real objects. But rational analysis, introduced too early and given too much emphasis, is unsuited to getting them to enjoy language and also leads to the neglect of concrete material.

Education that is *in accord with human nature* requires that a child be allowed to follow the same route in its mental development as did mankind in its thinking and investigating: that is from the concrete phenomenon to abstract laws. In contrast to that, we nowadays tend to start out from the models provided by science in order to take the child from the very beginning systematically through a quite specific approach. In this criticism I am in agreement with the educational reformer, Martin Wagenschein, who consistently demanded that *genetics courses* should start out from what is clear to the eye and can be observed without preconceived ideas, that is from the *phenomenon* itself, and only then go on to the possible laws behind them. This corresponds to the old educational requirement to give preference to inductive rather than deductive reasoning.

When training teachers I kept finding that the first idea that occurred to trainees who, for example, had to take the topic of 'forest' in a primary-two class, was to talk about the jungle, mixed woodland and monoculture, extracting individual trees versus clear felling, hydrologic balance and commercial forestry, the effects of climate change and pollution on the trees. But for children the forest is first and foremost a place that gives rise to quite specific feelings, a world of the uncanny, a setting for fairy tales, a world full of mysterious life and also a playground.

Years ago I took part in a kindergarten excursion in the forest. The parents and children gathered outside the forester's lodge at five in the morning and an ornithologist, who knew his material through and through, explained the birdsongs to the children. He went to a lot of trouble, but none of the children could tell a blackbird from a willow warbler and after five minutes they had lost all interest. Hardly surprising! For children of that age, the songs of all the birds on a beautiful May morning are a unity, a forest of sound, and it takes great skill to sharpen their ears so they can hear that there are different songs coming from various directions and distances. The psychologically correct way would have been to get the children to hear the bird calls as music and language. They could try to imitate various birds and suggest what they might be saying to each other. Anyone who thinks treating birdsong in that way will give the children wrong ideas that will stay with them for the rest of their lives, knows very little about the way children's minds develop. There is a right time for everything.

When I was training teachers, one student devoted his time to trying, through specifically designed questions, to get some idea of the way pupils of different ages saw the world. For our present purposes some of the answers he received from primary-one pupils on various natural phenomena and social conditions are revealing.

Manuela, asked why there is a full and a half moon, replied, 'Perhaps because of the weather. When it's a beautiful night, then there's a full moon, when it's not, there's a half moon.' That is children's logic: beauty is an expression of completeness, incompleteness goes with horrible things. Moreover the moon is not something alien, far away, it is a ball the size of which you can show with your hands, and the sun, because it shines more brightly, is slightly bigger.

The question that might embarrass some grown-ups — why the sky is blue — was meant *causally* by the student asking it, he was interested in the causes. That meant nothing to the child, however, she thought about the purpose of the phenomenon: 'It's so beautiful. Since the grass is green, there's no point in the sky being green as well. It's much nicer that it's blue.' Sibylle's answer to the same question is no less plausible: 'Because of the water, because afterwards the water comes down from the sky.' And if we adults believe the question why it rains will elicit a causal explanation from the child, we are wrong. The child naturally thinks in terms of *effect*: 'So things can grow, you see, if it never rained, things couldn't grow and we'd starve.'

When the student asked her what she particularly liked about her teacher, he assumed the child's way of thinking would be to detach individual characteristics or features from the whole person of the teacher. Sibylle's answer was totally disarming. What she liked most about her teacher was 'that she just comes back every morning, that we see her again.'

In general a seven-year-old child is no better at dividing its surroundings up into good and less good partial phenomena. Thus Sibylle answered the question as to what she liked best about her surroundings with almost Biblical simplicity: 'That I see my brother and my mother and my father.'

I must emphasise that these childish answers are neither second-rate nor stupid, rather they are based on a different way of looking at the world which one cannot automatically assume is inferior to the scientific view. When the student asked Sibylle how big she thought the sun was, she answered with a counter-question which might give some physicists pause for thought: '*With* its rays? With its rays it's pretty big. *Without* rays it's the same size as the moon.'

Even teachers are occasionally amazed by these answers. We all like to hear them because they reveal part of children's essential nature and that is a pleasure teachers can enjoy daily, provided we first let the children tell us what they think of certain things, before we begin with our explanation. Also, if the pupils see that we are interested in what they say and listen to them, they are more likely to return the compliment.

The change from magical-mythical thinking to reasoning along scientific lines does not occur at the same age in every child, nor at the same speed. And we can often see an intermediary stage between the above-mentioned thinking in effects and thinking in strict scientific causality. This intermediary stage — or preliminary stage of causality — consists of explanations on the model of: When it starts to get warmer in spring, the plants start to come up. When the moon's in the south at sunset, it's a half moon. When the water temperature sinks below zero, ice forms.

Naturally it is useful to familiarise oneself with this whole area by reading books on the psychology of development. But one cannot tell which stage a child is at from books, one can only establish that by observing the child carefully, especially by listening closely when it expresses its ideas on natural phenomena. This will give anyone teaching in the spirit of Pestalozzi fascinating insights into the world of the child; it will also fill them with amazement at the awakening of the spirit in a child.

'My method puts the ability to do common and necessary things far above the knowledge of unusual and superfluous things.'

17 **I Feel my Head's Going to Burst!**

The first thing I read as a freshly qualified teacher was a book called 'The Teacher's Card Index'. It was about collecting, keeping and ordering material. At that time it was not easy to get hold of good, suitable pictures and information, so one gathered anything that seemed at all usable — newspaper cuttings, pictures, brochures, postcards — and arranged it systematically in file indexes, envelopes and folders. And the teaching periodicals were shelved chronologically, perhaps even bound, but definitely with an index of topics kept on file. I am green with envy when I see what is available today.

But even today all that glitters is not gold. The flood of pictures and processed information in books, teaching packages, videos, films, schools' radio and television programmes is threatening to become an avalanche which will overwhelm us. Every subject area is dealt with. Top quality documentaries take us on adventurous expeditions to all four corners of the earth. Films on animal behaviour, plant life, ecological relationships and all aspects of the natural sciences bring the wonderful variety of creation into our living rooms. And then sound recordings: every piece of music is available, every language can be heard; works of literature are read by actors. On top of that the Internet as well — probably the most fantastic invention since the wheel. One can find information on anything and everything in no time at all. Millions of pages! Sometimes we really do feel our heads are going to burst.

In order not to drown in this flood or to simply take items on an arbitrary basis, a teacher needs sound criteria for choosing. Naturally some will say, 'What's that to do with me? I have my teaching schedule, I use the obligatory course materials and follow the head's instructions.' Others, however, may have found out to their sorrow that, using this strategy, they cannot quite complete the programme and have to proceed at a pace that does not allow them to deal with topics thoroughly. Such teachers take a more creative approach to their work and would like to put Pestalozzi's ideal of natural education into practice as far as possible. The considerations that follow are aimed at them, as well as at anyone who has influence on teaching schedules and teaching materials.

Fifty years ago schools still had a practical monopoly in the provision of basic general knowledge. What was available in the press and on the radio was seen as supplementary, as taking on from where school left off. But then television arrived, ordinary people started travelling abroad and finally the Internet gave the above-mentioned monopoly the *coup de grâce*. The question then arises whether there is any point any more in the school providing general knowledge that goes beyond what the pupils need for their everyday life?

One would like to be able to say, 'No, it's pointless, we'll reduce it radically and teach the pupils to use the Internet properly.' But it is not as simple as that, for it is impossible to cope with this flood of information on one's own without a relatively wide range of knowledge.

What should we do? I consider the following strategy right for this situation:

- First of all we must accept the fact that, under current conditions, the range of knowledge that the subject specialists and the producers of teaching materials and syllabuses seem to have in mind cannot be presented to and absorbed by the pupils in a way that is either educationally or psychologically correct. In every subject there are lots of attractive topics that simply have to be ignored. There is just no point in teachers and the devisers of syllabuses having a guilty conscience because not everything that is desirable can be done within the constraints of the current organisation of schools. 'Have the courage to leave gaps' is the watchword.

- The fact that modern mass communications have relieved schools of their monopoly in transmitting general knowledge suggests we should finally realise one of Pestalozzi's most important precepts, namely to place the acquisition of *skills* above the acquisition of *knowledge*. But we must be careful not to overdo it, since in the first place every skill is based on knowledge and in the second place one must possess some knowledge already before one can acquire more on one's own. At the least one must have some idea of what one does not know and of all the things one could know.

- We should aim for *quality*, not quantity. That is more easily said than done, especially when we consider the perfection in the presentation of knowledge by television. The lengths they go to simply in order to stimulate and retain the viewer's interest in a single documentary! The costs run into hundreds of thousands if not millions! Are we, battling away on our own, supposed to be able to compete with such perfect products in a geography or natural history lesson? No wonder the pupils are bored, they are used to different fare.

  The quality of the transmission of knowledge in schools must therefore lie elsewhere. We can, of course, use this or that piece of material these professionals have produced, but overall we must have different priorities. The strength of the school is that we can take the time to *lay the foundations* and that we *can go into the difficulties of individual pupils* — in brief, our teaching can be consciously *elementary*. That means a teacher will really get down to the fundamentals of a topic, first of all in his preparation and then in the presentation in class, and will deliberately go for depth, rather than breadth. In analysing the material he will separate the essential from the contingent and try to see the logic inherent in a topic to help the pupils understand it. This kind of elementary instruction is at the same time always *exemplary* in the sense that the basic concepts make it possible to understand related phenomena.

  One could object that my advocacy of this elementary and 'exemplary' learning, that gets to the bottom of things and takes a lot of time, is all well and good, but it does not provide an *overview of an area of knowledge*. The educational reformer, Martin Wagenschein, who has dealt with the subject of 'exemplary' learning in a manner that is as thorough as it is impressive, has also looked into this problem. As might be expected, he argues against going though a systematic course in the sciences and recommends taking a single phenomenon, which has a wealth of aspects that can be exploited, as the starting point for each unit. But even he knows that 'exemplary' knowledge runs the danger of being an isolated feature of the intellectual landscape. He therefore suggests joining the areas that have been dealt with intensively by *link-bridges* consisting of *brief surveys*, well aware that they will be pure — and relatively superficial — factual knowledge. I would like to illustrate this principle by applying it to the teaching of history.

Let us assume you have dealt with the European Middle Ages by the 'exemplary' method and taken the amount of time necessary, going deeply into the legal system of feudalism, the conventions of chivalry, the customs of courtly life, the way of life of ordinary people and the quarrel between the Emperor and the Pope. You have looked at medieval literature, art and architecture and, finally, at this or that war. If you were to continue in this way the pupils would be growing grey by the time you got to the year 2000. So, whether he likes it or not — and a history teacher won't like it, for the whole of history is close to his heart — the teacher has to start hopping about, perhaps stopping briefly at the Renaissance and the Reformation, then on to the Thirty Years' War or even straight to the French Revolution.

A pity, true, but there is no other way. So he has to copy Wagenschein's linking bridges: brief summaries, which the pupils have to commit to memory without having worked through them in detail. These sequences have little value in themselves, they are just a means to an end, lightly constructed arches to connect the load-bearing piers of the bridge. The best that they can do is give the pupils some idea of all there is to find out and to encourage them — since they could have developed a basic interest in history — to determine to go into it later on, when they have time.

- The appropriate use of the Internet will increasingly become part of teaching units, not only with regard to the actual topic but also with regard to pupils' proficiency in using the medium. We must, however, bear in mind that the total availability of all sorts of knowledge will tend to devalue *knowledge in itself*. Since people know that they could easily access a particular piece of knowledge, it doesn't seem worthwhile actually assimilating it. Thus there is the danger that they will merely extract short-term information from the Internet, but not commit themselves to making the effort to *familiarise themselves with an area of knowledge* under their own steam. Such knowledge that is extracted from processed information will remain superficial, will not really mean anything to them, and will in no way be comparable to knowledge that has been acquired through precise observation of the phenomena and committed study. Only this latter kind of knowledge will enable a personal view of the world to develop with a corresponding awareness. It is therefore sensible to observe a certain caution in using the facilities offered by the Internet.

- Finally, we must do everything we can to avoid pupils committing themselves to their work for the wrong reasons — for example simply to get a good mark. Knowledge that is learnt simply for the sake of the mark remains on the surface and quickly sinks back into the sea of oblivion. We must always be clear about our goal: we want to arouse *interest, the urge to know, to find out things*, to get the pupils to learn, to make an effort because it gives them *pleasure*. Anything that gets in the way of this is to be avoided. We have failed if even high-school students, who have come of age and qualified for university, make a point of burning everything that reminds them of, say, mathematics and physics after their final exams and swear never to have anything to do with them for the rest of their lives. We must question our grading system if we see that it prevents us from achieving the goals set out above. The huge expense in terms of personnel, organisation and finance that schools require today simply does not make sense if the system itself works against the most important goals.

'General mobility of the limbs and stamina in their various movements are the points of which elementary physical education consists.'

18 A Delicate Touch or the Big Fist?

Often you can hardly bear to look. You take advantage of a rainy day to go to a museum, this time not to look at paintings but at the art of the craftsman. In the display cases are the most delicate woven materials, fantastic products of the decorative art, as fine as spun gold — and we are told they were made from rye straw. What nimble fingers these people had — men, women and children! Yes, look the other way so as not to be reminded how weak, clumsy, ungainly all our wonderful technology has made us. Pestalozzi was right, faculties only develop with use. We become painfully aware of this in the area of manual dexterity. Advances in technology have largely taken over physical labour and manual skills in the rich countries of the West. Everything is easy, we don't have to lift a finger. But it comes at a price — at the expense of our manual dexterity and delicacy of touch.

Very early on schools, under Pestalozzi's influence, accepted that they should also develop the children's craft skills. Thus here in Switzerland, for example, there were 'manual dexterity lessons', as they used to be called, in which boys learnt first of all to handle paper, scissors, folders and knives, later on planes, saws, drills and chisels. Sometimes the course went on to include filing, grinding, polishing, soldering, repoussé work. And during their years of compulsory schooling the girls completed a collective apprenticeship in sewing and dressmaking, the best of them being well able to make their own clothes. They learnt all kinds of knitting, crocheting and embroidery as well, of course. And that was not the end of it. They learnt to cook, to furnish and decorate rooms, to run a household. The practical training of girls was seen as more important than that of the boys. There was a kind of second and third school for them beside the normal school: for work and for housekeeping. There were special colleges to train the teachers for this profession.

Single-sex education is a thing of the past now and the economic situation, which in the nineteenth century was the reason for the practical training in schools, has changed radically. Nowadays there is no economic reason for a young person to learn to knit stockings or pullovers, sew shirts, patch trousers, make cardboard boxes or bookshelves. As a result, the special courses, that took up such time and resources, have been replaced by other models: boys and girls learn the same and the goals in handicrafts, textiles and housekeeping have been changed and extended. Above all, however, the total time devoted to craft/practical subjects has been drastically cut.

This is not without its consequences. Most children do still learn to knit, but only a tiny minority develop sufficient skill to make it part of their lives. But at least they know about knitting and how it is done. The same is true of all the other handicraft techniques. The range of possible activities has been expanded, but in general the level of skill reached in the individual techniques is low. The reason is simple. Children would have to spend considerably more time learning a single technique and keep at it, practising properly until they had developed the desired degree of skill. That is tedious for many children, who have been spoilt and refuse to stick at the same thing for long, demanding constant variety.

Sometimes one finds well-equipped workshops for woodwork, hardly used any more, that have really just been left to go to rack and ruin. They are a symbol of the crisis in handicraft. It is clear to see, but it was also unavoidable, for the basic drive behind really good practical education has disappeared: economic necessity. That leaves us with the fundamental question of *what other motives can justify the teaching of handicrafts today*? I can see three.

Firstly: To a large extent technology has relieved us of physical activity and working hours have been reduced. That has led to a new problem, the organisation of our free time. Today many people pursue some hobby involving manual skill in their leisure time as compensation. It is helpful, then, if basic skills have been taught in handicraft and ideas for specific activities passed on. Among those are the classic techniques involving textiles, but also handling modelling clay, scissors, paper, glue and all the tools for artistic creation.

Secondly: The modern economy still has need of workers who are skilled with their hands. Good handicraft instruction can be useful preparation for this, not by anticipating specific aspects of an apprenticeship but by encouraging manual skill in general.

Thirdly: In these first two points, handicraft is considered with regard to its later practical usefulness. That was the reason behind the 'lessons in manual dexterity' and the 'work school' in the past. But the development of all our physical abilities, not just those of our hands, can and should be more, namely part of holistic education. This corresponds to Pestalozzi's view. Young people should enjoy an *all-round* education. The faculties that are developed should equip people to cope with any situation. It is not only our manual skills that benefit from good instruction in handicraft, it encourages other qualities such as perseverance, a sense of form and practical reasoning as well as precision and carefulness.

It is understandable that, given current attitudes, educational policy will emphasise the first two reasons and assess the quality of education according to its usefulness for the economy. It is, therefore, up to us teachers to take on the task of speaking out with demands for education that has the individual *as a full human being* at its centre and not just the needs of the economy. One of these demands concerns the development of the 'hand'. It is to the disadvantage of our development as human beings that it is unfortunately neglected in modern schools.

To what extent can the development of manual dexterity — not only in handicraft, but also in writing, drawing and painting — contribute to our development into full human beings? I see the following possibilities:

- As is well known, an infant first explores the world with its mouth but very soon with its hand as well. Anyone who uses their hand — from an infant to an old man — learns with every movement things that are important for life which do not need to be expressed in language. It is the hand itself which makes contact with the world, adapts to it and takes hold of it independently. When Pestalozzi talks of 'observation', he means the perception of the world with all our senses, including our sense of touch and movement. This is particularly effective in our hands. In this way our hand is also there in the 'observation' of the material world.

One example: Anyone who has never worked with modelling clay will find, when they first try it, that their fingers squeeze it clumsily, with no idea of the effect they produce, with no sense of the consistency, strength and malleability of the material. But their hands and fingers become increasingly more experienced, adjust to the reality of the material they are working with, adapt almost imperceptibility to its demands and possibilities and their idea increasingly takes form almost automatically. Our fingers are 'thinking' and acting themselves as they become more and more skilled.

- In using our hands we make what is perhaps our most important discovery: that not everything we can see in our minds is possible in reality. Our hand tells us what works and what doesn't. This practical work with our hands leads to *practical reason*, to a feeling for subtler but more important connections. It is not for nothing that superiors who started out with practical work have a better reputation with their workers than those who come from the theoretical side and often have little idea of what actually works or doesn't.

- It is the 'head' that is central to work in our schools and that has the great disadvantage that the pupils hardly ever perceive the results of their efforts with their senses — apart from marks. It is quite different with handicraft. There the success of their work is evident to their senses. Visible progress encourages them to continue their efforts which is a great help for pupils who lack motivation. *Perseverance* comes in a particular way in craft activities in that the stage the work has reached tells the pupil what has already been done and what is still to do. And when, finally, he can hold a satisfying or even good piece of work in his hand that will strengthen his *self-confidence* and his *self-esteem*. You only have to ask a bricklayer whether he feels inferior to an office-worker; he will tell you with pride that he gets pleasure from seeing the results of his work at the end of the day.

- Contemporary society has many names, one of which is *the throw-away society*. We don't just throw away things that are damaged, no longer usable, we throw away more or less anything, casually, as if it were nothing. Many people no longer feel any true *bond with their material possessions*. They are just props for the part we are playing at the moment and therefore quickly lose their attraction — so chuck them out! One has a true bond with an object when one knows its history, likes using or looking at it, looks after it and would be unhappy to give it away. Naturally it is difficult to feel such a bond with mass-produced industrial products. We feel closest to things which required some kind of special effort. At the very least that means care taken in choosing it, perhaps a high price, but that is nothing compared with the time and effort that goes into *making an object oneself*. By getting a child to make things himself in handicraft at school, we give him the opportunity to forge an emotional bond with material things.

   It is only the work of a moment to vandalise a stone statue on a fountain with spray-paint. But if children were allowed to work on a piece of stone with hammer and chisel at school and shape it into a simple figure, they would certainly not deface their handiwork out of pure boredom. Nor would they do it to their classmates' sculptures, unless they deliberately wanted to do it to spite them. The vandalism that is widespread today has its roots in the lack of emotional bonds with material objects, which leads to an inability to respect things to the creation of which others have devoted time and effort.

That brings us to the question of the principles it would be sensible to follow if we are to be successful in developing handicraft skills. Let us have a quick look at the way Pestalozzi saw things. He understands the development of these faculties as a four-stage process as well, though he stresses that the development of our physical faculties is *linked to that of our intellectual faculties* from the outset. This can be seen at the very first stage.

Pestalozzi calls this *first stage* 'attention to accuracy'. First of all the pupil should be made aware of what is important, of which movement and which way of using a tool is correct. As a rule that is done by the teacher demonstrating it, usually several times, starting slowly and pointing out the key factors at every stage. It starts, then, with a mental act.

Many teachers nowadays reject the idea that there is one correct way of doing things in the area of skills and allow the pupils more or less unrestricted freedom at this early stage. Generally, however, the result is that they get into the habit of using the wrong movements and the wrong way of using tools and have to put a great deal of effort into unlearning them later on, when they want or have to improve their skill.

The clearest example of this process is the way the pupils hold their pencils when writing or drawing. Children quite rightly start drawing and painting before they go to kindergarten; generally, however, no one shows them how to hold a pencil in a relaxed way. But that problem should be dealt with at kindergarten and infant school. If that does not happen, the impractical positions and movements will become fixed, resulting in those handwriting styles that are not truly personal, just clumsy. Naturally there are activities where it is appropriate to let a child get on with it without further instruction, but I believe it is wrong to make that a general principle, for the following reasons:

- Every skill such as writing, knitting, weaving, sewing, playing a musical instrument, using particular tools has been developed over the years or the centuries by specialists. Every technique, therefore, *represents a social resource* and success depends on following it. Also, every tool has been conceived with the appropriate use in mind, which puts relatively narrow limits on its employment. Putting tools that are possibly even dangerous into children's hands without preparation and simply telling them to be creative has nothing to do with freedom and imagination. I see no reason why the regulations controlling the use of a chisel, for example, should not apply to all tools — including writing implements.

In the area of leisure activities this Pestalozzian basis is accepted as a matter of course. Take a first golf lesson, for example, or watch the children at ballet class. I therefore find it even more difficult to understand the resistance I occasionally encounter from colleagues when they are asked not to let the children write letters or numbers the wrong way round and to show them the correct way to hold writing implements.

- Teachers who love children take their childish urges seriously and respond to them, but that does not mean we must always accept them. Rather, we take them seriously by dealing with them openly. Granting these childish urges absolute validity encourages an *asocial attitude*. The child will begin to believe he only has to accept things that spring from his own desires. But the world and society — not just ours, every society — quite justifiably make demands which individuals must be able to conform to. If a young person does not learn this, he will attract attention for the wrong reasons at the very latest when he starts an apprenticeship. There he will have to stick to quite specific techniques without argument for reasons of safety, quality and efficiency.

At Pestalozzi's *second stage* the child imitates the teacher and tries things out for himself. Very often he also needs to acquire the physical strength needed for the sequence of movements. Pestalozzi calls this phase 'strength to produce'. The teacher should keep a close eye on the pupils as they do this and point out mistakes in the imitation of the desired movements. Thus when a child starts learning a musical instrument, for example, one should not leave him to practise alone, but do so together with him until one is sure that he is not reinforcing mistakes during practice.

The *third stage* is concerned with dexterity, agility, with what Pestalozzi calls 'lightness and delicacy of movement'. It is the stage of patient, persevering practice. Through it the child increasingly integrates the skill into his own being. He gradually starts making the sequence of movements correctly without having to think about it. He can feel himself in each of his movements and they are successful. This is the development of the 'observation with the hand' I talked about at the beginning of this chapter.

The *fourth stage* is the stage of 'freedom and independence'. The learner has reached a certain degree of 'mastery' and that means two things. In the first place he can use the skill he has acquired to realise projects he chooses himself because he likes them or because they are important to him for other reasons. If, for example, he has learnt to play a musical instrument, he can now choose himself what he will play; if he has learnt woodworking techniques, he can decide what objects he will make. In the second place mastery means that, should he feel the need, he can develop the technique in a way that suits him. Thus this fourth stage is the stage of true creativity.

It is to be welcomed that in handicraft we allow the imagination and creativity of the individual pupils much greater scope than in the past. The problem with this is that we are in danger of losing any sense of external constraint, of everything becoming a matter of 'just please yourself'. The constraints the pupil will come across as he learns to apply a technique or to use a tool will prove a necessary counterweight to that. The technique comes from society and is therefore — naturally within sensible limits — determined; the content is the expression of individual creativity and therefore free. In this synthesis of models that are produced and handed down by society and the individual's own creativity, the pupil will experience a paradigm of one of the fundamental aspects of our existence as human beings.

In this chapter on the development of craft skills I have deliberately placed great emphasis on careful attention to techniques and the proper handling of tools and materials. In that I was conscious of following Pestalozzi's principles. I was also trying to counter the widespread low regard in which craftwork is held. There is a constant supply of new factors to back up this disparagement:

- All modern machine-made products are characterised by a high degree of perfection and therefore often seem very impersonal, cold and dead. There is a reaction against this, especially among the younger generation. As a counterweight people cultivate the incomplete, preferring things that are unfinished, imperfect, used, worn. One only needs to look at the current fashion in dress! Advertising also relies on the effect of the incomplete: drawings that look as if they were done by a child and handwriting that is as clumsy as possible are used to suggest spontaneity, liveliness, genuineness. It is thus natural for a teacher simply to enjoy the poetry of the incomplete and not exasperate his pupils with demands for greater care and precision.

-   It is not only fashion and advertising that cultivate the incomplete, fine art does so as well. That is not a value judgment, for neither the rejection nor the cultivation of perfection tells us anything about the real substance of a work. The rejection of perfect detail has been with us since the Impressionists at the latest; the Action Painters were probably the ones who took it farthest. Anything that is thrown or sprayed onto the canvas quickly and with passion seems spontaneous, refreshing, expressive. It does not just liberate the artist, it also liberates the observer, leaving him free to make what he likes of the work. Some sculptors reject perfection as well, attacking the clay furiously or using a chain saw. I do not dismiss that, for 'art' has its own laws. The simple fact is that a significant part of the visual arts has rejected and still rejects perfection and that this development has had its effect on what happens in school today: care, precision and delicacy are hard to find. In the past a fuss was made when a pupil blotted his exercise book; nowadays if one of these painters lets paint that is a little too thin dribble unintentionally over the picture, he leaves it — chance made the decision for him.

-   In some respects even Pestalozzi did not take children as such entirely seriously. He saw them primarily as beings that needed to be educated with regard to their full humanity and the tasks awaiting them as adults. Consequently too little attention was paid to childish playfulness, childish imagination and childish spontaneity. It is only in the twentieth century that children have been taken seriously as children, that the intrinsic value of childhood and childishness has been recognised. Even in this, however, it is possible to go too far, as happens when no limits are set on children's selfishness and a laissez-faire attitude results in absolute trust in children's powers of self-development. In this context, the idea that children must also accept and acquire social norms has a hard time of it.

Do not get me wrong. I like modern art and take pleasure in the poetry of incompleteness and the spontaneous expressions of children before they have been educated. There is a place for all that. When we first give children clay at school we should be happy to leave them free to find out what it is like for themselves. When we give them finger paints they should daub them all over the paper like an Action Painter. But when they have a pair of scissors in their hand, I want to show them how to use them so that they do not poke anyone's eye out and get the best result they can. And in making a pot I would not rely entirely on their spontaneity but would show the clumsier ones, if they do not realise it themselves, that they must not press too much or too little when rolling out the clay. I want to avoid flaws appearing after the pots have been fired because air got into the clay. And I don't want a child to be frustrated when a beautiful vase he is making slumps just as he reaches the neck because he did not strengthen the join between the bottom and the sides properly. Or to put it as a principle: I think all one-sidedness is wrong, in everything I look for a synthesis between tradition and innovation, between freedom and constraint.

The title of this chapter is the question: 'A delicate touch or the big fist?' It reflects my opinion that someone who has developed a delicate touch will be more likely to stroke with his hand than clench it into a fist. But I am clear that what I hope will be the end product of education — full humanity — cannot be achieved by one-sided training of the hands, but requires all-round education. Part of that is practice in the way to resolve conflicts, which is what I want to look at in chapters 20 and 21.

'O man, your organism is the organism of a sensory shell in which a divine being rests and lives.'

19 What is Man?

How about a little philosophy? In this chapter I would like to present the philosophical standpoint on which my book is based. It has become important in my life and has helped me to order my thoughts and understand human life better.

What is man?

Like every true thinker, Pestalozzi wanted a sound intellectual foundation for his political proposals and campaigns, and especially for his educational theories. For him, that meant to be clear in his mind about the 'nature of man', about 'man in his essence'. His reflections and observations went so far that he had no qualms about calling himself an 'authority on human nature'.

Pestalozzi developed his anthropological ideas in his philosophical magnum opus, *Meine Nachforschungen über den Gang der Natur in der Entwicklung des Menschengeschlechts (1797). (My Investigations into the Course of Nature in the Evolution of Mankind)*. I will summarise its main ideas below.

Man's Twofold Nature

Unlike animals, which are always in harmony with themselves, man's existence is marked by *tension* and *inner conflict*. For Pestalozzi, the reason lay in man's twofold nature, the two sides of which he called 'animal' and 'higher' human nature.

Our *animal nature*, also often called our *sensory nature*, comprises all those aspects of our life which serve our own survival and that of the species, and which tie us to our physical bodies and our sensory system. It drives us to satisfy our needs and makes us seek pleasure and avoid pain, feel all sorts of feelings such as like and dislike as well as prompting us to indulge our lethargy and selfishness.

Our *higher nature* makes possible those things that raise us above the animals: our ability to recognise truth, practise love, believe in God, listen to our conscience, exercise justice, develop a sense of beauty, recognise higher values and act on them, be creative, act in freedom, bear responsibility, overcome our own selfishness, develop communal life, follow the dictates of reason, seek to improve ourselves. Pestalozzi was convinced that a 'divine spark' manifested itself in this human potential, which made man into an image of the divine. He therefore often also called our higher nature our 'inner', 'eternal', 'spiritual', or 'divine' nature.

These two sides of human nature are different in essence but they are bound together in their appearance, since our higher being is rooted in our animal nature and grows out of it. Thus it is the task of education to raise our animal-sensory nature as far as possible to the higher level. He recognises the value of our lower nature, as long as it does not impede the development of our higher potential.

Pestalozzi's Investigations

The view of human nature set forth here runs through the whole of Pestalozzi's thought. It was mainly in his writings after 1800 that he expressed it with such clarity but it is also the basis of the idea behind the *Investigations* mentioned above. Starting out from the experience of inner conflict and the question of its origin and purpose, he came to the conclusion that human life takes place in three different 'conditions'. These are three different modes of existence, each with its own laws, namely the *natural condition,* the *social condition*, and the *moral condition*. In the first two it is our animal nature that is dominant, and in the moral condition, our higher nature.

The Natural Condition

The natural condition is regulated by two opposing drives: *egoism*, serving the self, and *goodwill*, directing the self to others. Within the framework of social life, goodwill can be mixed and can even have a destructive effect — for example when it appears as naive good nature — but it is the natural basis for our morality, for it is from goodwill that love gradually emerges.

Within the natural condition Pestalozzi distinguishes between the *pure, uncorrupted* form and the *corrupted* form. In the *uncorrupted natural condition* our needs and the powers we have to satisfy them are permanently in *balance*. We do not want more than we are capable of and what we are capable of is no less than what we need. We abandon ourselves to the pure enjoyment of the senses and enjoy unthreatened security. Everything we do is directed towards the moment; we are unconcerned about the past or the future. There are no obstacles in the way of our egoism, it serves our survival alone, which no one contests or makes difficult for us. Egoism and goodwill are in harmonious balance. We are without guilt, for we obey our natural instincts, which have not yet been corrupted. No one hampers our natural urge for freedom so that it does not turn to violence.

In this idea of uncorrupted, natural man it is not difficult to see Rousseau's picture of the noble savage, a picture, moreover, which even today has lost none of its seductive power. But Pestalozzi draws a clear distinction between himself and his spiritual forebear in emphasising that the uncorrupted natural condition is not something of which we can have direct experience. It vanishes with 'our first cry', for that is audible proof of the disproportion between the infant's needs and its actual powers. The uncorrupted natural condition is a construct of *thought*, but that is what makes it effective, because it allows us to *imagine* the lost harmony we seek to recover. Of course, Pestalozzi realised that this purely natural harmony based on instinct is of necessity irretrievably lost to us. There is no return to animal simplicity, free of problems. Our lost harmony must be restored by other means — by morality freely accepted, as we will see later.

The direct experience we have of man as we know him is of the *corrupted* natural condition. By that Pestalozzi understands man as a creature of instinct and urges, a self-centred 'animal'. In this corrupted natural condition the balance between our desires and needs and the powers required to satisfy them has been lost. In contrast to our situation in the uncorrupted natural condition, we find ourselves to be weak, inadequate and in need of help, our lives characterised by fear, exertion, struggle. As long as no one gets in our way, we are still full of goodwill, for that is in line with our lethargy and the fact that in general we feel more comfortable in concord with others than in dispute. Since, however, our daily worries arouse our egoism, we all more or less seek power, which results in a struggle of everyone against everyone else. Individuals — as long as they are still in the corrupted natural state — have no compunction about forcing through their desire for power and possessions at others' expense. They claim the right to 'natural freedom', that is to do whatever they like, if necessary with recourse to violence.

The Social Condition

We find a first solution to the trials and tribulations of the corrupted natural condition by entering the social condition. Pestalozzi examines the *process of socialisation* from two aspects. Firstly, he sees it as an irreversible historical event lying far back in the past and characterised by the invention of property, with all its consequences, in particular the creation of 'positive law', that is law that supersedes natural law. Secondly, he sees 'socialisation' as a process that is happening all the time as individuals, now reasoning beings, become aware of their corrupted natural being. The corrupted natural condition is only distinct from the social condition *in theory,* for the egoistical struggle for power and possessions in the corrupted natural condition assumes the existence of property. In this situation the concept and regulation of property are 'social', but the selfish, ruthless pursuit of one's own interests at the expense of others' is 'animal'. Since in our everyday experience animal selfishness and property are almost inseparable, and since in our selfishness we resort to all available social means, including positive law, in the pursuit of our own interests, Pestalozzi also called the social condition the *modified natural condition*.

Let us remind ourselves what it was that brought about socialisation in the first place. We sought security and an easier way of satisfying our needs by collective means, above all by acquisition, possession and the division of labour. It is the task of law to regulate this and to apportion the fruits of socialisation to everyone.

Now it is a fundamental aspect of law and therefore of every social order, that to secure the individual's rights it must *impose duties* on him and curtail his *natural freedom*. This leads to conflict within ourselves, for our entry into the social condition has not eliminated our egoism. The same egoism that motivated our socialisation, in order to enjoy its advantages, keeps causing us to try and shake off the consequences of that step. The result is that in the condition of socialisation we can never achieve the purpose for which we entered that condition. We become socialised in the hope of recovering the lost harmony between our needs and our powers, and it is precisely that harmony that we can never achieve in the social condition. On the contrary, the social process arouses more and more new needs while at the same time making the individual less and less free by its ever more complex dependencies, and more and more weak by the increased division of labour and reduction in the skills demanded of him.

Since when we are socialised *and nothing more* we are anything but reliable socially, the social state is always unstable. Its quality depends on the extent to which it is regulated by just laws and the extent to which individuals keep to those laws. If we — as lawgivers, rulers or simple citizens — respect social justice, then we help to stabilise the social state and create the conditions that will allow the individual to rise to morality. If, on the other hand, we disregard the laws and social justice, we undermine the social condition and are in constant danger, as individuals, of sinking back into the animal condition. We will, to quote Pestalozzi, become tyrants, slaves or barbarians.

It is unthinkable for Pestalozzi that we should be satisfied simply with becoming collectivised and civilised, not least because the social condition is in no position to guarantee fulfilment to the individual. Despite that, the social condition is unavoidable as a necessary intermediate stage in our progress from the natural condition to the moral condition. The thing that distinguishes the social condition from the natural condition is our ability to keep our instinctive reactions in check, even if only as a response to social pressure. This habituation to *external obedience* to the laws is a prefiguration of our *inner obedience* to our own conscience. In fact everything we suffer under the conditions and contradictions of the social condition has a deeper meaning. According to Pestalozzi, we must feel the deficiencies of being united merely on a social level 'deeply for as long as it takes' for us to recognise that our lost harmony can only be re-established when we grasp the opportunity of moral freedom and desire good and our own wholeness of our *own free will*.

The Moral Condition

With that we rise to the *moral* condition. This rests on the independent power within us, on the 'divine spark'. Thanks to this power, which in its essence is independent of the animal and social conditions, we can *make ourselves whole*. In Pestalozzi's own words: *I* [he means human beings in general] *possess a power within myself to present all the things of this world to my inner self, independent of my animal desire and my social circumstances, entirely from the point of view of what they can contribute to my inner improvement, and to accept or reject them according to that point of view alone. This power is independent within my innermost being and in no way the consequence of any other power of my nature. It exists because I exist, and I exist because it exists. Its source is the feeling present in my innermost being that I can make myself whole if I let what I ought to do rule what I want to do.*

This independent power is, however, quite individual — '*it is not shared with anyone else*' — and therefore morality is individual as well, for '*no one can feel: "I am" for me; no one can feel: "I am moral" for me.*'

For Pestalozzi, therefore, morality is not external to us, something that expresses itself in good social institutions, just laws and the tradition of good habits. Morality is always the action of our individual will resulting from a free decision of our conscience and can be recognised from the fact that in performing it *we freely overcome our own egoism.*

It is only through this moral will that we can re-establish our lost harmony with ourselves and overcome the contradictions within ourselves because our will is directed towards what reason and conscience tell us is necessary. Through such a free, moral act we become *'our own creation'*, we become 'human beings' in the true sense of the word. And to become a 'human being' is the foremost and essential task and vocation of each of us and we will continue to suffer under the contradictions of our nature, under the imperfections and demands of society until we come to recognise that it is we ourselves who are responsible for a fulfilled existence.

Morality, then, is entirely bound to the decision of each individual. No one can make a person moral apart from that person himself; other people and social conditions can only make this easier or more difficult or suggest it. Amongst other things, Pestalozzi wrote: *For me the only purely moral motives to do one's duty are those which belong entirely to my individuality. Every motive to do my duty which I share with others is not moral; on the contrary, it is in the nature of such motives that they always tempt me to behave in an immoral way, that is not to see the deceptiveness of my animal nature and the injustice of my social hardening. The greater the number of those with whom I share my duty, the stronger and more varied the temptations to immorality which are connected with that duty... All the things I do as a member of a group, of a community — even more the demands I have to make as a member of a guild, a party, always dehumanise me to a greater or lesser degree. The larger the group, the community, the guild or the party, from which my rights and duties derive, the greater the danger of dehumanisation, that is social hardening against all the claims morality makes on that duty and those rights.*

Banding together to realise one's own interests, which are proclaimed as good, may produce some welcome social changes, but according to Pestalozzi such collective action has nothing to do with true morality.

Nothing could be more wrong than to accuse Pestalozzi of asocial individualism because of this. The fundamental aim of morality — to achieve wholeness by overcoming our own egoism — is essentially social. Pestalozzi cannot imagine morality in any other way than as the individual's personal devotion to others and to the community in active love. Beyond that, it is precisely through our individual moral actions that we have a constructive effect on society.

His unequivocal call to us to live a moral life does not make Pestalozzi a utopian dreamer. He freely admits that it is *impossible* for us to act in a *purely* moral way since we are permanently involved in society and are also natural creatures with urges and needs, the satisfaction of which must take priority over moral action if we are to survive. Thus Pestalozzi clearly accepts the inner conflict and tension that is part of our nature. Inner peace and harmony with ourselves and the world can never be something we possess permanently, it can only be something we experience with each new act of our own will.

The Application

Pestalozzi's philosophy makes us aware that all essential phenomena of human life (for example power, freedom, peace, conflict resolution, marriage, occupation) in fact have *three meanings*, which are contradictory because our natural, social and moral lives *are each subject to different laws*. What is appropriate to one condition could well be in conflict with the laws of another. *Power*, for example, — as institutional power – belongs to the social condition, which could not survive without it, but it is of no use in arousing moral life. Similarly *suspicion* is a must in society, without checks everything would get out of hand. But in our personal lives, which should be based on the morality of those involved, suspicion is corrosive.

If we are not conscious of this, there is a danger that in any debate we will fundamentally misunderstand what others are saying. This happened in the eighties of the last century in the discussions on peace. Whilst some had the peace of a polity in mind, i.e. a value belonging to the social condition that had to be defended if the worst came to the worst, others were talking about a concept of peace that was based on the Bible and therefore connected with the moral condition. Their in part absolute demands were founded on their belief in a 'pure morality' which, according to Pestalozzi, we human beings can never possess.

The same kind of thing happens in the often very impassioned discussions within the church, in which love and power are seen as opposites without the participants realising that *every* institution has to work within a power structure and the love of the individual belongs in a very different context. With his philosophy Pestalozzi is suggesting we should on the one hand recognise that contradiction is an ineradicable part of human life, whilst on the other attempting — as far as is possible in practice — to abolish it in our own actions.

Pestalozzi himself illustrates the threefold nature of human acts with various examples and I will take the one from *religion* here. As *natural* beings we respond to the numinous with fear and make physical images of God and the world beyond. The *social* aspect of religion appears in religious communities, each with its own customs, norms and power structures. Religion is only truly *moral* as a personal consciousness of the divine, as an existential response to the divine experienced within oneself. But it is typical of Pestalozzi — who knows that *pure* morality is impossible – that he does not reject the natural and social aspects, despite the clear hierarchy of value in this threefold view. On the contrary, he sees them as means of 'steering us towards' the moral, though only as long as the means do not hinder the end.

Pestalozzi's Philosophy and Education

It follows that teaching can also be analysed using Pestalozzi's theory of the three conditions. Our professional work is also subject to the inevitable contradiction:

As *natural* beings we want our work to be enjoyable, to be as easy as possible to carry out and to bring us recognition and financial reward.

As *social beings* we have a contract which on the one hand grants us rights and power (for example the simple right to work in the school and earn our living), and on the other puts us under obligations, for example to keep to the school hours, to get through the syllabus, to see that the school rules are obeyed, to take part in promotion procedures and selection mechanisms, to continue our professional development and to observe all the statutory requirements.

It is only the *moral aspect* of our work that provides real fulfilment. We contribute to the overall progress of the children in our care towards full humanity by developing their faculties while respecting them as persons, by opening up their senses, introducing them to the variety of the world and doing all we can to help them grow up into good people. No one can order us to do this and the more all-embracing the quality assurance systems that are introduced, the less will we produce that quality which rests solely on the moral freedom of the individual.

In Pestalozzi's 1815 book, *'To the Innocence, Seriousness and High-mindedness of my Age and my Fatherland'*, the difference between the social and the moral was at the centre of his analysis. He contrasts 'collective existence' and 'civilisation', which belong to the social condition, with the 'individual existence' and 'culture' which characterise the moral condition. For our purposes it is significant that he insists that education and upbringing in general unquestionably belong to individual existence.

If we look at the present situation in schools and the changes that are currently taking place, it is unfortunately clear that developments are going in the opposite direction. The purely social (entrenchment behind legal and institutional requirements and therefore standardisation and the reliance on power) is becoming ever more dominant in the educational sphere, threatening to smother what Pestalozzi understands by culture. Consideration of individual factors, for both teachers and pupils, goes by the board and with it the measure of freedom which is indispensable for fruitful educational work. The teacher's relationship with pupils is becoming increasingly strained. The more we teachers have to carry out legally ordained measures, which run counter to the pupils' wants, needs and wishes, the more they will see us as enforcers of an anonymous machine instead of as helpers who understand and engage with their individual personalities.

Naturally the organisation of compulsory schooling is unthinkable without social regulation. However, those who regulate it ought to be clear that it should be a *framework* which should allow the real business of schools — education founded on a moral community and aimed at developing the morality of all involved — to proceed on the basis of freedom and personal commitment. Different laws operate in the education of young people than, say, in road construction. There the state itself can *effect* the full realisation of its projects, and that goes for all other areas that are concerned with perfecting things or systems. But that does not work with schools. There the educational administration and educational policy cannot *effect* anything, they can only make it possible or, unfortunately, more difficult.

The realisation of the wishes formulated by the state is always the responsibility of those directly involved: teachers and pupils. However much energy is put into perfecting, or at least modifying, systems, results will only improve when those involved are determined that they will improve. And they will be all the more determined, the less their freedom and their scope for creativity is curtailed and the less they are reduced to the role of executive functionaries.

'What is a life embittered by envy and hatred, quarrels and disputes, child? The hours of love, of gentleness and peace, they alone are hours of life.'

20 **Let Him Have It!**

Playtime. Four boys have surrounded Luke, escape is impossible. He knows he's in for it now. 'Let him have it,' one of the boys shouts and the blows rain down on him. What has he done? Stupid question! He's just Luke, the dimwit, the fatty with the squint, the big baby. He knows what violence means.

The bell sounds — end of playtime. Luke creeps back into the classroom, quietly crying.

What happens next? There are three possibilities.

Teacher A: 'Open your atlases, page 27.'

Teacher B: 'What's wrong with you? Have you been in a row again? It's always the same.' *Luke*, 'They hit me again.'

Teacher B, 'Well you'll just have to learn to defend yourself, otherwise you'll never grow up to be a man. Open your atlases, page 27.'

Teacher C: 'You've been crying, Luke. Something's wrong.' *Luke*, 'They hit me again.'

Teacher C, 'Again? It can't go on like this. Put your atlases away. Get your chairs and sit round in a circle here.'

Teachers earn their coffee break; after all, teaching is demanding and tiring. And playground supervision usually works. Fortunately not all our colleagues share the view that we shouldn't interfere in children's arguments. 'The children will sort it out themselves. They need to learn to look after themselves.' If you want to know where that leads, you only have to look at a chicken run. The law is clear: the strong rule the roost, the weak keep their heads down.

It is true that there are many places where bullying at school or on the way to and from school has not become an issue. But in many other places it has, and a very serious issue at that. Fights are a regular occurrence, and the boys don't just use their fists, they kick and even hit their opponents right in the face with knuckle-dusters, unconcerned about injuries they might cause. And even worse, today they have worked out how the Mafia operates, extorting protection money or little services. And after the money's been handed over: 'Don't you dare tell on us or you'll really be for it.' So some remain silent, while others lord it over them.

And the girls are following suit. The spread of such behaviour is a new phenomenon, which leads us to the question of how it could happen. The answer that the social environment has changed is true, but too general. I see the following factors:

- The system that for centuries required and supported moral behaviour has almost completely lost its effectiveness: the Ten Commandments from the Old Testament. Even fifty years ago the spirit and the letter were binding for children and adolescents. Not wanting to fall into sin was definitely a motivation to eschew violence and show consideration to others. That is largely a thing of the past.

- It is definitely connected with this, that our society has turned into a dog-eat-dog society. The slogans are: 'Look after number one.' — 'Get on.' — 'The end justifies the means.' — 'Might is right.' — 'If you get hurt, that's your problem.' Naturally not everyone thinks or behaves like that, but there are too many who set that kind of example. And young people simply lap it up.

- The range of the mass media has grown beyond all imagining. However many of those involved in production behave in a responsible manner, there will always be many others who will do anything for money. Consequently we have a mass culture in music, television, computer games and the Internet which is characterised by aggressiveness, violence and brutality. Regular, or even addictive immersion in such scenes cannot be without effect.

- Sport, too, has to a great extent lost the element of play. The idea of fairness, in which winning is secondary to observing the spirit of the game, has largely fallen by the wayside. More and more brutal martial arts are invented. Clearly people still regard it as sport when one participant kicks his opponent as hard as possible in the face and knocks him unconscious. It is enough for one person to be a supporter of the other team for another to beat him senseless. Given the huge number of young people whose only interest is sport, this culture of violence associated with it sets a disastrous example.

- Our society has not managed to assimilate the many immigrants from other countries and cultures. I am not trying to point the finger at anyone, simply to note that in the context of ethnic conflict individual readiness to resort to violence becomes collective. There is little that education can do about this, since individuals who refuse to join in violence may suffer sanctions from the group they belong to.

As a result there are — quite rightly — calls for the *prevention of violence*. These are directed first and foremost at parents, but schools are also expected to contribute. If I were to be asked what schools can do to prevent violence, my answer would be short and sweet: the whole concept of education presented in this book *is* violence prevention. It does not make sense to organise schools in a way that ignores psychology and the demands of the learning situation, with the result that they become a breeding ground for violence, and then to think the problem can be solved with a few supplementary measures. On the contrary, teaching must be organised in a way that allows the school as a whole to lay the foundations for living in a community that is free of violence. In practice this means that the syllabus must take second place to building up a sense of community. Classes need to be stable communities that foster the gradual development of a network of emotional relationships. We need institutions that are on a human scale, so that the individual pupil does not get swallowed up in the mass and lose all sense of responsibility. We need lasting relationships between teachers and pupils who know each other and take each other seriously. And we need enough time so that the conflicts, that occur daily, can be resolved in a way that is psychologically and educationally correct. The division of teaching time into 45-minute periods, the excessive use of subject specialists (which may be justified at secondary level), the concentration of senior pupils in large campuses, the constant regrouping of pupils in different-level courses for the individual subjects (comprehensive school), the reduction of teachers to simple organisers — all that has a tendency to favour the emergence of violence. We must finally stop education going in the wrong direction.

It is a serious problem, which affects not just our schools, but the whole of society. If we do not give the resolution of conflicts precedence over the material of the syllabus, the potential for conflict will continue to rise until it comes to the point where we have no idea how to deal with it. The atmosphere in society will be marked by a lack of consideration for others' points of view, by argument, fighting and violence. All our finer feelings — sympathy, affection, understanding, helpfulness, friendship — will be blotted out. Learning will be no pleasure, merely a response to pressure and threat; at best it will satisfy the ambition of the good pupils.

A few more words on the *resolution of conflict*. First of all it is important to be aware that the squabbles or outbreaks of violence we encounter are not the actual conflicts but attempts — unsuitable attempts, it is true —to resolve the conflict. The actual conflict goes deeper, smouldering, latent, always seated within the emotions. Fears, feelings of aggression, resentment, hurt, disappointment, inferiority all feed and dominate the conflict. In the surface disagreements these feelings pressurise and determine our behaviour.

Seen from the perspective of Pestalozzi's three modes of existence, violent clashes are the resolution of conflicts in the *natural condition*. Each of those involved uses the means of power available to him to force through his opinions or intentions. It starts with subtle manipulation, continues with argument, which can be anything from clever to obstinate, intensifies in psychological pressure and ends with naked physical violence. The result is always clear: the stronger one wins.

Institutionalised strategies for the resolution of conflict in the *social condition* have been devised to prevent this war of everyone against everyone else — at least as far as physical violence is concerned

— in order to protect the weak. They can avail themselves of the power of the society to receive what the law says they are entitled to. The one with right on his side wins.

When resolving conflict in the *moral condition,* we get to the bottom of the true causes of the conflict by taking the whole situation of the individuals concerned seriously. We all engage with the feelings, needs and concerns of those involved, forgo selfish advantages and make every effort to meet the others in understanding and love and find a creative solution. There are no losers because all are in favour of the solution that is found.

Conflict resolution in the moral condition is only possible in relatively close personal relationships. They are part of our 'individual existence'. Collective conflicts of interest cannot be resolved on this basis, but are a matter for the social mechanisms of conflict resolution. The aim of both the moral and the social resolution strategy is to prevent or replace the strategy based on the right of the stronger.

Schools — in which teaching is on a personal level, but which, as public institutions, are subject to the rules and regulations of the social condition — also have the task of replacing the pupils' attempts at conflict resolution based on personal power with solutions on the moral or social level.

Moral conflict resolution concentrates on the *education, the mental and psychological growth* of the individuals concerned, while the social concentrates on *protecting the weaker members.* As far as the problem of violence is concerned, the moral strategy aims at *prevention*, the social at *suppression.* That is always necessary when for whatever reason prevention does not work. And since, as we know from experience, prevention does not always work, it is unavoidable, if regrettable, that we must resort to punishment or other measures provided by law to set limits.

For teachers that hurts, which is why we persevere with prevention for as long as possible. And that consists of permanently cultivating conflict resolution on the moral level. From the outset we abandon the idea that we must find the guilty person and punish him. What we are looking for is mutual understanding and solutions for the future. We refrain from using our power, but what we do require is the teacher's authority. That comes from taking the pupils seriously, from acting in a way that is based on the values we proclaim so that they trust us as individual people. Discussions that are conducted in that spirit can not only resolve the conflict in question but can also bring all those involved closer together, which will improve the general atmosphere and lead to a constant reduction in the sources of conflict. There is, therefore, no need to fear that learning will be adversely affected by putting the development of the community first. The opposite is the case.

This is where Thomas Gordon comes in with his 'no-lose method conflict resolution'. He has become well known through his books *Teacher Effectiveness Training* and *Parent Effectiveness Training* plus other writings of similar import. They are all based on the same principle: conflicts should be resolved in such a way that there is no winner or loser. No one should emerge victorious but every one should be a winner — a winner in terms of quality of life and humanity. But that is only possible when our feelings — our own and the pupils' — are taken seriously.

But we must also recognise the limits of this method: fundamental to it is the assumption of the good will of all those concerned and that is not just important, it is the decisive factor. Unfortunately, it is often very difficult if not impossible to arouse good will in adolescents who up to that point have enjoyed the success of their physical superiority. The only thing capable of relaxing such a permanently truculent posture is a strong personality with convincing authority, which is founded on love and speaks directly to the heart of a young person like that. Otherwise that leaves just the measures on the social level, in order to protect the others.

Perhaps the day will come when people will recognise that what the world lacks is not people who are well informed, but people who are well brought up. Then our schools will be organised in such a way that they can educate children to help them develop into full human beings. And then children like the Luke mentioned at the beginning of this chapter will no longer have their lives made a misery.

'Love is the first thing that anyone who fears for his life forgets.'

Well Meant and a
21 **Complete Failure**

In the previous chapter I showed what makes for the right resolution of conflict. And yes, I do have the audacity to describe a solution as right or wrong. What I regard as *wrong* is, firstly, anything that goes against the intentions of the person in charge and is thus a clear failure; secondly, anything that increases the problems instead of reducing them; thirdly, anything that is contrary to basic ethical principles. *Right*, therefore, is anything that is felt to be successful, anything that solves the problem — assuming it can be identified — and anything that can be justified from an ethical point of view.

Here I would like to discuss an attempt at conflict resolution which a teacher wrote up afterwards and which I regard as wrong. The example is from a collection which was put together by a group of researchers at Zurich University at the beginning of the seventies. Their aim was to clarify the real 'educational needs of teachers' and they invited teachers in Zurich to think about everyday life in their own schools and to send in anonymous descriptions of 'critical situations demanding a decision'.

Before I start I would like to apologise to my unknown colleague for using an action which he took spontaneously as a response to a professional challenge as the subject of a theoretical discussion. My excuse is threefold: in the first place the 'case' is such a classic example of a teacher with the best of intentions doing what he thought was for the best and yet failing because the theories his action was based on were wrong, that I could hardly find a better one. In the second place I am not passing judgment on the unknown teacher, simply on the 'case' as we find it in his description. To do justice to the teacher as a human being I would have to be acquainted with him and let him have his say. And in the third place I have to confess — may God forgive me —that I made much worse mistakes in the early years of my career. I assume it was the same for him as for me: with increasing experience we learn from our mistakes and gradually find the path to the truth.

The teacher's report:

'Rolf and Fritz are the weakest pupils in the class. They have both had to repeat a year but still find it difficult to follow the lessons. The two of them were accused by their classmates of having smoked cigarettes in the woods during an orienteering run (setting off from different points in groups of four). I discuss the incident with the class. It is not so much the fact of smoking that is criticised (almost all of them have smoked at some time or other) as the way they had shut themselves off from the rest of the class and not joined in the game. The class decrees that the two boys should miss the next outing and stay in school doing written work under the supervision of one of my colleagues.

That evening Fritz's mother rings me up and explains that Rolf had bought the cigarettes and her son was not to blame. His classmates had told her about the incident. I explain that both boys have to be reprimanded for their behaviour. Since, however, I knew that Rolf had too much pocket money, I rang his mother and recommended they check he made sensible use of it. The next morning there is a violent knock on the classroom door. Rolf's father is there, angry and ready for an argument; in a rude tone he asks what is going on. His son, he says, was forced by Fritz (who threatened to beat him up otherwise) to buy cigarettes. I tell him that the matter is closed as far as I am concerned. Now Rolf's father starts complaining angrily that his son has been unfairly treated. Pointing out that this is neither the time nor the place for a discussion, since it is disrupting teaching, I reject his complaint and object to the tone he has adopted. That only makes Rolf's father even more angry. Turning to leave, he shouts that he will see me outside if it doesn't suit me here.'

What immediately strikes one about this is that by the end the whole problem is much more complicated than at the beginning. The relatively minor matter of two boys smoking a cigarette in the woods has grown into a situation that can only be sorted out with great difficulty: two boys are banned from the school outing, their relationship with the class has been seriously impaired, the two boys and their parents are now at loggerheads with each other, the accord between the teacher and the parents of the two boys has been destroyed and the affair threatens to end up before the education authorities. All this is a clear sign that the problem was approached in the wrong way.

From the few details given we can deduce that the teacher was trained in the sixties, at a time when in educational circles the slogans 'democracy in the school' and 'the classroom as a practice ground for democracy' were current. In line with that, he 'called a public meeting' to solve the problem — at least superficially — and turned the classroom into a court of law, as is indicated by the expression *'the class decrees...'*

There are objections to that on two levels, on the one hand to the *way it was carried out* but also — and above all — to that *method of resolving conflicts in itself.*

The model the teacher is using as a guideline is the process used against people who break the law, roughly following the sequence: crime or misdemeanour → report to the authorities → investigation → charge → trial, including defence → guilty verdict → sentence → possibility of appeal → sentence carried out → possibility of a pardon.

It is not by chance that our example omits all provision which formal legal proceedings have *in favour of the accused*: a proper investigation, defence, the possibility of appeal and pardon. In my opinion that expresses the unconscious attitude of the teacher and the class towards the two boys: basically, they were found guilty as soon as the offence was reported and all that was left was to find a punishment that would hurt in order to show them who's boss. It has also clearly not struck the teacher that in proper legal proceedings those who report a crime and are directly affected by it cannot be judge and jury, and should certainly not — as happens here — profit from the sentence. The two boys have had to repeat a year and that makes them what we might call foreign bodies in the class, that is, they are socially marginalised. Their classmates would prefer not to have them with them on the school outing. The punishment that was 'decreed' speaks loud and clear.

The excessive punishment also gives one pause for thought. The two are being forced to miss the best thing in the year, the school outing. Instead, they have to do what they are least good at (*'Rolf and Fritz are the weakest pupils in the class'*) and probably hate most: written work. On top of that they will have to appear before another class as miscreants. It seems to me that this kind of punishment says little about the degree of guilt but a lot about the degree of rejection they suffer from those who have condemned them.

On the basis of what one can glean from the report, I also suspect that, although they are hardly aware of it, there is an alliance between the teacher and the class against the two boys which means on the one hand that the pupils unconsciously meet the teacher's expectations and on the other that the class decisions are protection for the teacher. That is a form of power against which one can do nothing and which therefore makes Rolf's father's feeling of outrage understandable. In general there is a certain coolness, a certain distance about the teacher's language (*'I explain that both boys have to be reprimanded for their behaviour'* — *'...recommended they check he made sensible use of it'* — *'I tell him that the matter is closed as far as I am concerned'* — *'Pointing out that this is neither the time nor the place for a discussion, since it is disrupting teaching, I reject his complaint and object to the tone he has adopted'*) which could be seen positively as expressing superiority and strength, but which comes across to the others as the exercise of power and makes them feel correspondingly impotent. Nowhere is there a sign that the teacher might have any understanding for the feelings of others, nor does he show the faintest sense that he might have made a mistake, even that he himself might be responsible for the worsening of the problem.

For these reasons I consider the method the teacher chooses to be fundamentally mistaken. In order to show the alternative method, I have concocted a fictitious conversation about this example between Heinrich Pestalozzi, Alfred Adler, Ruth Cohn and Thomas Gordon:

Pestalozzi: My friends, I'm sure you have read my *Investigations*, in which I demonstrate that 'democracy' does not entail the renunciation of power but is, in fact, a form of power structure. It is therefore quite clearly situated in the social condition, which is why its mechanisms —

for example legal proceedings — are out of place in all situations which must be shaped from the perspective of the moral condition. Or do you take a different view, Herr Adler?

Adler: Not at all. I have spent my whole life pointing out that the exercise of power arouses, in those who are its object, feelings of inferiority, for which they then compensate by exercising power themselves, with the result that conflicts are aggravated, as we see clearly in our example. I suspect that the two boys smoked the cigarettes in order to make themselves seem big and grown-up — at least to each other — that is, out of the unconscious desire to compensate for their feelings of inferiority by seeking prestige and superiority. The teacher does not seem to understand this, for the process he orders or allows only increases the two boys' sense of inferiority: they are shown up by having to stand before the class as accused. And the particular punishment makes them feel very clearly that they are not wanted.

Gordon: I can only agree with you, Herr Pestalozzi, Herr Adler. Personal conflicts cannot be resolved by the use of power, for that always creates winners and losers.

Cohn: That is also the reason why I do not get the participants to vote in my method of theme-concentrated interaction. Voting, that is deciding by a majority against a minority, is all right within the state, since there is no better way. In a school class, however, there is mostly a better way, and that means that 'democratic' procedures are out of place there. When conflicts arise in a community we have to go to the trouble of looking for a solution together for as long as it takes until everyone involved can agree. Admittedly that is often difficult, especially at the beginning. But when all the members of the group regularly find that their feelings, needs and desires are taken seriously, they become increasingly ready to engage with the others and to put selfish attitudes behind them. The teacher in our example was quite right to involve the whole class in solving the problem, and it is to be hoped that this becomes the rule. But he ought not to guide the discussion so that it concludes by finding someone guilty and punishing them.

Gordon: The important thing would be for every pupil to look inside himself and then to say what *his* experience of the situation was and what *he* had felt at the time. Pupils of that age are perfectly capable of formulating genuine I-messages if they are shown properly how to do so. This ability would be encouraged if the teacher were to listen to all of them — especially the two 'miscreants' — genuinely, that is 'actively'. Then the two boys might pluck up the courage to tell their classmates what was going on inside them when they decided to smoke. Only on that basis is it possible for that kind of discussion to reach its goal: not, namely, to point the finger at and punish the guilty ones, but to bring understanding and help for the future.

Cohn: To come down to practical matters, I would get the pupils to sit in a circle, of which I would also be part. Then I would start by telling them to ask themselves: what was my experience of the orienteering run? If this form of discussion had been practised in class, they wouldn't express suppositions about others but truly examine themselves and give genuine answers. Rolf and Fritz would then also have the opportunity to say openly how they felt.

Pestalozzi: That is the spirit of the moral condition: we genuinely seek the truth and do not depart from the path of love, even when not everything turns out as we would wish.

Adler: Precisely. It's all about developing a sense of community. That is only possible when power is left out of it and we support each other with help.

Gordon: That is why I ... I wouldn't say 'invented', rather I discovered the 'no-lose method of conflict resolution'.

Pestalozzi: I'm sure you're right about that. In education we can't invent anything, everything we do — the whole 'art' — must be derived from human nature. Our example is proof that the teacher's way of dealing with problems was not in accord with human nature, for it created revolt and rejection. I am convinced, Herr Gordon, that with your method, which I was unfortunately not acquainted with during my lifetime, you will eventually achieve general agreement and love will return.

Cohn: Not only that, understanding will grow as well and only then can the problem really be solved. It must have become clear that the problem was not simply the two boys' smoking — or their lack of interest in the athletic side of the exercise, as the teacher puts it — but the social rejection of the pair. Thus all of them, teacher and pupils, are involved in the problem and therefore have a duty to make a contribution to solving it.

Adler: And that's why this punishment is so wrong as well. It obscures the fact that this conflict is a problem concerning *all* of them and completely *discourages* the two boys while aggravating the real problem, their social isolation. We must bear in mind that all the experiences they will have on the school outing together will form a bond between the pupils, and these two, who are being punished, will be excluded from these experiences which will strengthen the sense of community. What is needed is the opposite: the two boys must be *encouraged* by the fact that the class has recognised the real problem and takes it seriously. And that will only happen if in future they feel they are more part of the community, that they are *accepted*.

Gordon: What this shows is that every conflict has a deeper meaning. Conflicts bring sore points out into the open and if they are properly dealt with, everybody is a winner.

Adler: Correct. And what is gained is an increased sense of community in everyone. It is only in community that we human beings become good human beings...

Pestalozzi: ...which shows that 'community' and 'society' are not the same. 'Community' is always a question of the interplay between the natural condition and the moral condition, and that means contact between one human being and others. 'Society', on the other hand, views human beings collectively and is not really interested in them as individuals.

Gordon: Yes, and when you talk of individuals, that does not mean just the pupils in our example, but the teacher as well. The great tragedy for him is that he thinks he has to have everything under control and can't show his own feelings. The kind of resolution of the conflict we are proposing here would be a relief for him too. He feels he has to fight against everyone and everything. That isolates him and turns people, who could well be kindly disposed towards him, into enemies.

Adler: This aggressive attitude comes out clearly in his cool defensive reaction to Rolf's father's outrage.

Gordon: I have to admit that such situations require great presence of mind. But if the teacher had realised that every angry outburst is a clear sign that a person feels completely impotent, he could — instead of reprimanding him — have shown that he understood his anger.

Cohn: Yes, disruption is what this is all about and it is not sensible to send the angry father away because teaching must not be disrupted.

Gordon: If he had learnt to listen actively, he would perhaps have said, 'I can see that something has happened to make you very angry and you want to sort that out with me.' Then the father would have sensed that he was being taken seriously and would have offered to clear the matter up calmly at another time.

Pestalozzi: Of course, the important thing is not the choice of words, but the spirit that comes out in them. Words are just so much noise if they are not imbued with real humanity, with truth and love.

'The heart alone can guide the heart.'

How Can We Manage
22 Without the Cane?

It was easy to maintain discipline with the cane in your hand. The little rascals knew all about the bruises and weals, so they behaved themselves. The bad old days!

And today? This really happened: a pupil hands in a sloppily written piece of work, the teacher asks him to rewrite it and the pupil says, without batting an eyelid, 'You'll have a long wait.' The bad new days!

This example is by no means exceptional, worse things happen every day. How can one teach under these circumstances? Schools, which are legally required to deliver the syllabus, can only function if it is not just the teachers who comply by taking their task seriously, but if the pupils in particular do what is asked of them.

In many classrooms today we are suffering the consequences of the anti-authoritarian movement of the late sixties and early seventies of the previous century. What started off as justified criticism of any form of oppression ended up as absolute criticism and rejection of power in any form. And the authority quoted is Jakob Burckhardt with his statement that power is *inherently* evil.

They could have quoted Pestalozzi as well: *It is not power, it is the person who wields power who is responsible for the corruption of the human race. Everything that flows from power is sacred and good, as long as the person wielding it is faithful, his word an honest word and his faithfulness as steadfast as the steadfast stars.*

What is power? It is simply the *potential for one individual to subject the behaviour or the fate of another to his own will.* If I choose the topic of 'guinea pigs' it is the *fate* of my pupils to be confronted with the life of these charming animals. And I subject their *behaviour* to my will by telling them to have a good look then try to tell me what they can see. What is wrong with that?

In other words, the teacher must have undisputed power in order to do his job.

But how does this fit in with my argument that using one's power in trying to resolve conflicts is counterproductive and Gordon's 'no-lose method' of resolving conflict requires one to set one's power aside? The answer is simple: *only someone who wields power can decide not to use it.* It is, anyway, impossible for an inexperienced teacher with a disruptive class (which existed in the past just as today) to try and resolve the mass of conflicts that threaten to overwhelm him in the first five minutes by Gordon's method. What do you do, if you shout above the noise that they should be so good as to sit in a circle so that you can all discuss problems together, and they thumb their noses at you or, as a sign of their contempt, take all the papers out of your folder and scatter them round the room? It quickly becomes clear that you are lost without power. That was the reason why, when training teachers I advised my future colleagues, when we were studying Gordon's methods, to forget not using power until you've actually got it. As teachers we do not refrain from using our power because it has been snatched from us but because we realise that children develop better in conditions where power has been replaced by a sense of community. To refrain from using one's power one must be free to use it.

Let us return to the above-mentioned chaos. In such a precarious situation teachers in the old days could compel the respect of the class with the cane, or something similar. That is a thing of the past now, I'm glad to say. Today we need *power without the cane*, and that means *authority*. And that was the case in the old days as well; a teacher with authority had no need of the cane.

Which brings us to the question: What is authority? We teachers possess two kinds of authority, which must be clearly distinguished. As holders of an official position we are part of a legally defined institution and thus share in the power that goes with it. This *institutional power* appears, as far as pupils are concerned, in our right to demand things of them, to assess and mark their work and to require them to observe the school rules. But the pupils couldn't care less about such legal niceties. What is important for them is what they actually see in the person of the teacher. To the extent that they feel obliged to follow his instructions, they are responding not to his institutional, but to his *personal* authority.

Personal authority is something of a mystery. Two people can stand in front of a class and use the same words to instruct the pupils to do something; in one case they will obey as a matter of course, whilst in the other they will behave as if they had not heard anything. The effectiveness does not, therefore, lie in the words themselves, but in the force that lies within them and emanates from the one who spoke them. This force is connected with the aura a person gives off and to which children and adults react spontaneously. This aura tells us something about the person's credibility, trustworthiness, competence, strength of will, reliability and seriousness. Usually we react to it within a few seconds, either with acceptance, indifference or rejection. This reaction has something to do with resonance. If a person's appearance and bearing sets something resonating in others, he will become an authority for them, a person they take seriously, obeying his expressions of will. And they do this without feeling oppressed. Genuine authority does not oppress others, on the contrary it leads them, they are uplifted by it.

Here is an example. At a school camp a trainee teacher noticed that some boys were constantly teasing and tormenting another and excluding him from their games. He quite correctly spoke to them about their behaviour, tried to get them to understand the feelings of the boy who was excluded and appealed to their consciences, but with resignation he concluded, 'Hardly had I turned my back than they were teasing him again, as if I hadn't said anything.' What he lacked was real authority, his words carried no weight with the children.

This shows us the way genuine authority works. As Goethe said, we humans are creatures with 'two souls in our breast' — one that encloses us within ourselves and makes us into egoists, and one that raises us above ourselves, sending us in search of what is good, of our true selves.

169

This will, I am sure, be the case with those 'bad' boys: in certain situations their behaviour is antisocial, but each of them bears within him the potential to understand others and treat them with consideration, in brief, the potential for good. And here we can see the effect of genuine authority: *It is by genuine authority (and by that alone) that the good forces in the child can be helped to gain the upper hand over the less good ones.* Genuine authority awakens and strengthens the child's self, helps him to be and become himself.

We teachers want more than just momentary successes. We are not satisfied — to return to our example —with the excluded boy being left in peace or integrated in the group. We want all those involved to grow through the conflict and to develop an attitude which will have a positive effect in other situations. To quote Pestalozzi, authority aims to reach the innermost core of the person, its goal is to bring out the powers of the heart. Empathy, trust, courage, gratitude, a sense of justice and of community are to be developed.

Of course, authority is not a quality one does or doesn't have; one person has more, another less. From Pestalozzi's point of view, authority is a faculty that can, like any other faculty, be *developed.* Consequently the degree of perceptible authority is always a blend of natural talent and deliberate cultivation. If the natural talent is great and the corresponding cultivation as a moral force lacking, authority can be dangerous. It enables its possessor to fill people with enthusiasm, to lead people, but it can also enable him to lead them astray, if what he fills them with enthusiasm for is bad. History has plenty of examples. The lesson therefore is: the greater the natural talent for leadership, the more important its cultivation as a moral force — and that means the development of a sense of responsibility.

As far as the cultivation of authority is concerned, I consider the following points essential:

- First of all one must have the courage to believe in one's authority and to put it to the test. If one loses it, one must leave the profession. The best intentions, the most conscientious preparation, the most ingenious ideas, the highest ideals are ineffective without authority. It is the soil in which everything thrives.

- That is why, as teachers, we should react especially firmly to anything that undermines our authority. However, we get into a circular argument here — or is it a vicious circle? — that is impossible to break out of: to be able to deal convincingly with actions that diminish our authority we need to possess a high degree of authority, otherwise the pupils will not take our response seriously.

- Since genuine authority demands self-confidence and a healthy degree of self-esteem it is essential for teachers to make that part of their personal development.

- Beyond that, there are a number of techniques one can use to bolster one's authority which one can bear in mind and consciously employ: when speaking, a teacher should make a point of maintaining eye contact with the whole class and not continuing if they are not paying attention or talking amongst themselves. He should take care to speak clearly and understandably, and his whole bearing and expression should emphasise his authority.

- Equally, there are ways of behaving which diminish one's authority, though I will not go into them in detail. It is sensible to avoid embarrassing the pupils.

Now it is true that there is a type of authority that the pupils feel is simply a demand to be obeyed. True authority, therefore, always goes together with *love of children*. Modern educational theory tends to avoid discussing this basis for fruitful work as a teacher. It almost seems as if it is taken for granted that everyone feels affection for children or that it has no relevance for education. It is true that some effects of this basic attitude — for example 'engage with the child' or 'always be polite' — are demanded, but that is behaviour which can, if necessary, be acquired by practice without that mysterious something — love of children — being alive in the teacher. In Pestalozzi's view of mankind, love as the basis for the development of our moral faculties cannot be reduced to a few behavioural practices. It is, rather, a mental and psychological reality beyond any specific situation, which is still a living presence even if there is no interpersonal contact at the moment. Love supports our sense of responsibility, our capacity for understanding, our desire to work, our self-criticism and our willingness to tackle difficulties and overcome them.

But we must distinguish between two forms of love: Love for children in general and love for the individual child.

To anticipate any possible misunderstanding — the affection for children that is under discussion here has nothing to do with sexual love. It is about the teacher as a person being open to children's nature as such. It is comparable to the attitude of a person who is open to the fascination of a wild flower in bloom and stands looking at it in wonderment, pondering, while others pass by unnoticing. A teacher who loves children is open to the spontaneity of burgeoning life in a child, to its imagination and creativity, which keep appearing at the most surprising moments, to the workings of a mysterious force of development, indeed, to the mystery of life itself which reveals itself in children in ever new ways. Such a teacher can therefore never be bored by children. Deep down inside he feels himself a kindred spirit and is thus always on the child's side when its childish nature is in danger of being crushed by the harsh realities of life.

It is precisely this love for children that makes teachers aware of children's weaknesses and the dangers they face, for their love is not sentimental. It is, to quote Pestalozzi, a 'seeing' love. Such a teacher is well able to distinguish between genuine childish naivety and artful coquetry. He knows the difference between obstinacy, which always appears when a person wants to refuse something that is necessary or gain an advantage at another's cost, and independence of mind, which is an expression of a person's innermost being. He would never regard pupils who were overexcited as 'lively' or take their bluffing, their cheap imitating, for creativity. Nor would he confuse forwardness, precociousness and a craving for recognition with self-confidence and healthy self-esteem. And, finally, he would not wrongly interpret cheekiness and uncouth behaviour as honesty, nor the fear of engaging with something new as strength of character.

Love for children always expresses itself as affection for the individual child the teacher is dealing with at the moment. Thus he feels not only the duty but also the need to see the child as an individual, as a unique, unrepeatable personality. It is, of course, necessary to pay attention to each child's *performance in school work*, but a loving teacher will not stop at that, he will also *recognise the child as a person* and learn to see him as he really is. We can only do that if we accept him as a human being and are interested in his individuality, his circumstances, his likes and dislikes, his talents, his state of development, his thoughts and feelings, his weaknesses and his difficulties. All that is part of what Pestalozzi calls 'seeing love'. This comprehensive perception of the child enables the teacher to get inside the child, to come to him with understanding and to assist him in his difficulties instead — as so often happens — of confronting him with punishment.

This approach often meets with the objection that it is impossible to expect teachers to like all pupils equally since we, too, are subject to feelings of sympathy and antipathy. That cannot be denied, for we are only normal human beings. However, we discover from experience that feelings of sympathy and antipathy very much fade into the background when we succeed in truly *understanding* a person the way they are. The question, though, is: what should we do to get our understanding of a person to grow? I am convinced that *open dialogue* is one of the fundamental requirements for that. In this respect the art of guiding a discussion, as Thomas Gordon teaches us, for example, is of great importance for a teacher. If we can *listen with empathy,* our liking for the person opening themselves up to us will grow.

As a rule, love is returned. The younger the children, the more they are prepared to make an effort to please the teacher. The aim of all this is naturally not to get the children to work hard just to please the teacher; they should commit themselves to their work because they realise it is right or simply because they find it rewarding. But with younger children it is a very human motivation to try to win — or, even better, respond to — the teacher's love through their hard work and the effort they put in. In so doing, they will develop an interest in the subject and pleasure in a neatly done piece of work. And that will stay with them later on when they no longer do it to please their teacher, but from their own motivation.

The love we are talking about here is not simply the legitimate partner of authority, it can also strengthen authority or even serve as

173

a basis for it. There is an impressive example of this in a report written by a seventeen-year-old trainee teacher: in the summer camp he was helping to run, one boy stood out because of his grumbling and blatant disobedience. Whatever orders the leaders gave, he ignored them. One morning the children were told to get ready for a day out walking with their hiking boots and waterproofs. The 'notorious grumbler', as he appeared to be to the leaders, set off in trainers and even left his windcheater behind. And, sure enough, the weather did get worse in the course of the afternoon, which gave the senior leader the opportunity to savour his triumph: 'Now do you see that you should follow our orders. If you won't listen you must take the consequences.'

That was certainly not a bad thing the leader said and there are enough educationalists who, following Rousseau, would do the same — we learn from our sufferings. The snag is that it doesn't work, for the simple reason that this 'teaching by logical consequences' lacks love.

The student felt sorry for the poor lad and lent him his pullover — which, in the eyes of the leader, was acting contrary to good educational practice. This meant that the two of them got left behind a little and the boy told the student his whole life story, with all his worries and problems, and from that point on he obeyed the student unquestioningly and did whatever the other asked of him.

To avoid any misunderstanding, I must point out that I do not maintain that the student's behaviour as described here would work in every case and independently of the people involved. I am also well aware that it would have been better if the leaders had checked that their instructions had been obeyed before they set off. I simply wanted to demonstrate the connection between love and authority.

To conclude this chapter on the teacher's love of children I will look at an extended quotation from Pestalozzi. This passage, from the final version of his novel *Lienhard und Gertrud* (Leonard and Gertrude), describes the teacher, Glülphi, after he has become acquainted with Gertrude's teaching in accord with human nature: *As soon as he entered the school the very next day, he forgot his dream, the world and all his desire to improve the world and people. He was once more heart and soul the schoolmaster with nothing in mind but this moment in which he stood among his children as father and teacher... In these hours of work he was completely absorbed by their presence, as if there were nothing in the world apart from his children round him... As they gathered together, Glülphi no longer saw his children as a group. Each child appeared individually, and when he saw, or even just thought of a child, his being was entirely concentrated on him or her, as if there were no others around... Thus he bore all the children of his school in his heart. That also meant that, day by day, he knew precisely the stage each one was at in his teaching. Every day he looked more deeply into the heart of each one and with every day he became more familiar with all their thoughts and endeavours...*

The cane no longer has any place in classrooms where the teaching is in that spirit. But modern education still brandishes the cane, a very different type of cane, it is true, but one that hurts just as much as the old one: the system of giving marks. I would prefer not to have this system in our schools but to see it replaced by a more sensible one. Pestalozzi himself was against it, and for very good reasons. Already I can hear people ask in astonishment, 'But how are you going to get the pupils to really work instead of sitting around doing nothing?' It is a question that must be taken seriously and my answer comes from this chapter: by the teacher's authority that is rooted in love. If he presents the material in a way that is appropriate to children and brings it alive, he will motivate his pupils to learn and to work, without having to threaten them with marks.

'Language without observation is inconceivable, observation without language unfruitful, and observation and language without love does not lead to that which makes the education of our race human.'

Thirty Periods a Week of German — 23 or Any Other Mother Tongue

The best way for anyone to get an idea of the linguistic competence of mainly young people would be to look at all the Internet sites where they chat away and — because of the spontaneity of the way they express themselves — reveal their limited linguistic ability. It is widely recognised to be a problem: not only instructors, especially on commercial courses, complain that their apprentices left school without a proper command of German, university lecturers make the same complaint about their students.

One could let the matter rest there, pointing out that everyone manages to struggle through one way or another. But as educators we simply cannot accept this. We have a twofold task: to identify the causes of this disastrous situation and to find suitable means of addressing it.

There are doubtless many causes and in part they come from influences outside the education system. That is not under discussion here. In schools it is, in my opinion, the currently dominant theory of language teaching that is partly responsible. It puts too much emphasis on the positive effect of understanding of and knowledge about language to the neglect of letting pupils get into the habit of speaking and writing correctly through persistent practice. But I also believe that a not inconsiderable factor in this unfortunate situation is that the whole burden of developing language skills falls on German teachers with very few hours at their disposal. This comes from our habit of putting everything into little boxes, of organising teaching along the lines of the division of labour in an industrial concern: everyone has his subject and no one should interfere in someone else's territory. But it is not interference we are talking about, it is *collective responsibility.*

That is why I mean the title of this chapter seriously. The thirty or so periods a week pupils have, ought to be used to improve their language skills *as well.*

Already I can hear an objection. 'That is all well and good, but if I follow that the pupils will tell me to my face, "What has my pronunciation, my grammar and spelling to do with you? We're doing Geography here, not German." ' That is a problem, but at least we should realise what the basic attitude is that makes pupils react in that way. They regard school not as an aid organisation but as a battlefield. Their aim is to resist any avoidable exertion and to see that they do not have to change unless it is really necessary. And this attitude is only possible because the pupils have not identified with the most fundamental educational aims of school. They see the syllabus as something imposed on them from outside; but if they saw it as guidelines to a goal they themselves wanted to achieve, they would be grateful for any hint on how to improve their oral and written expression.

But it is not the unsatisfactory results of our education system alone that justify the suggestion that the whole of the school staff should be responsible for developing language skills. The grounds for it lie deeper. Every subject is dependent, among other things, on language and that implies a responsibility which every teacher, whatever they teach, has to share.

Language is the intellectual house we all inhabit. It is intimately connected with thought. Both, *language* and *thought,* rest on the same foundation, on the concepts integrated into our consciousness which we link together according to the laws of logic. Thus a correct sentence always corresponds to a clearly conceived thought. And since thinking occurs in all subjects, we are all responsible for seeing that the pupils do learn not just to think correctly, but also to express themselves with corresponding clarity.

Thus every teacher, whatever subject he teaches, has an opportunity to help develop language skills where it is a matter of clarity of expression. The pupils should be made to feel the close relationship between thought and language. If I were a mathematics or physics teacher, my pupils would have to formulate every logical relationship, every conformity to a law of physics, in comprehensible sentences before they were allowed to express it in a mathematical formula. I would not be satisfied, however smoothly the pupils could recite 'a plus b all squared equals a squared plus two ab plus b squared', they would have to be able to render this mathematical formula in language from their own understanding, not just because they had learnt it off by heart.

However, language is not our intellectual home simply because it allows us *to get a mental hold on the world*, to grasp it and comprehend it with our thoughts, but also because it makes *communication* with other human beings possible. And since communication takes place in all subjects, speaking correctly can be practised in all subjects.

A wide *vocabulary* and the ability to express oneself *in grammatically correct form* is the core of linguistic competence. But that is by no means the end of it, for that core has a suit of clothing, as one might say, in which it appears to listeners and readers. In speaking, this outer layer consists of *articulation and all rhetorical modes of expression*, in writing, of *correct spelling and punctuation*.

The cultivation of these two aspects of linguistic competence is at the heart of language teaching, but the goal — the ability to write and speak correctly — is so hard to achieve that it is beyond the German teacher unless the other subject teachers support him or, where there is one class teacher, he makes it part of every subject. It does not make sense at all for pupils to take care over grammar, spelling, punctuation and the choice of words in essay writing but to be allowed to break the rules as much as they like in their other subjects. Schools as a whole must insist that the central aims of the individual subjects should be observed across the whole range of pupils' work.

How can the ideas I have put forward here be put into practice in the classroom? I see three main ways:

Firstly: We must create as many opportunities for speaking as possible and teachers and pupils must concentrate on speaking correctly.

Particularly useful is *free discussion among pupils*. This is appropriate whenever the pupils must *discover things for themselves*, as well as for any exercise involving observation, describing pictures, expressing opinions on problems and interpreting texts. A teacher's mastery can be seen in the way he trains a class in the rules of free discussion.

Secondly: Correction by the teacher. Unfortunately the view is widespread today that correcting pupils makes them feel hurt, discourages them and increases their sense of inferiority. That attitude kills two birds with one stone: you're one of the good guys and at the same time you've got rid of the most onerous of a teacher's tasks. If this attitude becomes general we needn't be surprised about the poor results of education and we can happily dispense with all our quality assurance systems.

Admittedly, correction can have a hurtful, discouraging effect, but that is on a quite different level, on that of the teacher's emotional relationship with the pupil. In an atmosphere of acceptance, it is quite possible, even in primary one, to put in a second 'n' if the child has written, say, 'funy' without upsetting him. And when the child is told to write the word again, he will understand it as it is meant, as help. In our leisure activities we quite happily accept our mistakes in a movement or way of doing something being pointed out and being asked to do it properly; it is only in school that it is looked upon as morally reprehensible.

Outside the language classes it is essential that mistakes in *written work* be corrected, especially in science subjects. No teacher would think of letting the mistakes in language, which he points out to the pupil by correcting them, affect the mark given.

Just as important, however, is correction in *oral work*. Here the art for the teacher lies in making as little fuss as possible over the correction. I have found it works well simply to say the correct word or phrase, almost as an afterthought, even following the pupil's tone of speaking. The pupils had got into the habit of repeating the correct version and then continuing with what they were saying. Mostly they didn't even notice that I had corrected them.

Thirdly: Setting a good example is essential. For a teacher, improving one's own linguistic competence is a lifelong task: ensuring that one's vocabulary is vivid, comprehensible and varied, one's sentences are correctly formulated and clearly pronounced.

In this connection I would like to discuss two forms of teaching which are somewhat looked down upon by modern educational theory: 'chalk and talk' and storytelling. In both cases the teacher's language serves as a model.

'Chalk and talk' is the original form of teaching: someone who knows something tells it to others who would like to hear it or need to know it. This form of teaching has its advantages and can produce positive effects. Necessary information and connections can be conveyed very efficiently. Also the pupils are repeatedly given a model of how problems are analysed, judgments made and knowledge presented.

Storytelling presents unique events which the pupils could not find out for themselves by discussion or through the exercise of logic. Someone — the teacher or a pupil — knows about something and passes on their knowledge.

Storytelling has been criticised. For some educationalists it is problematic that the teacher is at the centre and makes the pupils' minds dependent on him, pushing them into passivity. I do not accept this criticism. A person who is listening, transforming words into mental images, being emotionally involved is just as active as the person telling the story. The speaker and the listener are in an equal relationship, neither is at the centre, the centre is the story, to which both have given themselves up.

Telling a story and listening are truly elementary. For thousands of years people of all races have used storytelling to pass on to the next generation traditional knowledge that is considered vital. It is not surprising, then, that children respond particularly well to storytelling and usually put off any other activity if they can listen to someone telling a story in a way that is both geared to children and exciting.

Many children today do not like going to school, and the older they are, the greater their resistance. In my opinion the reason lies in the fact that schools place too much emphasis on the intellectual side — what Pestalozzi calls the 'head' — and neglect not only the 'hand' but also the 'heart'. Good storytelling always appeals to the emotions. Educationalists who would like to banish storytelling from the classroom, or marginalise it, must be clear that with that we would lose one of the main opportunities to appeal to the children's emotions and thus arouse their interest and make them willing collaborators in the learning process.

During the last twenty years of my work training teachers I repeatedly found the positive effect of storytelling confirmed. When the trainee teachers first arrived, at the age of sixteen, I regularly asked them for their assessment of the history teaching they had had so far. The unfortunate truth was that there were only very few who had enjoyed it and had developed an interest in history; and they were always those whose history teacher had been a person who regularly recounted fascinating stories.

My recommendation to teachers in all subjects, then, is to take every opportunity to tell a story that will capture your pupils' interest, and not just at infants level, but in all classes. That will not only add spice to your own teaching, through its example it will also contribute to 'language training in all subjects'.

'A person who combats his own urges will be eternally rewarded with the consciousness of a higher, inner strength.'

24 Can EUED Make You Ill?

The question of whether EUED itself is a disease I will leave to the experts, but one thing is certain: EUED *can make you ill*.

It is a serious matter. It concerns the way we use television, computers, the Internet, mobile telephones and other electronic devices and the content of mass communication. In a certain respect they are all part of a single phenomenon: people *immersing themselves in an artificial world with the help of electronic technology*. For that reason I think I am justified in dealing with the whole area as a unity. It will be easy for the reader to infer at any point which medium my arguments are specifically directed at.

What is indisputable is that, to live in our society, young people must familiarise themselves with computers and the Internet. They should learn as early as possible to use a keyboard properly, not just with one or two fingers. They should be able to find useful information and use electronic technology to solve all kinds of problems. That is relatively straightforward and simply a matter of sensible planning.

But as teachers we are faced with the problem of how this new technology can be *used constructively* and how any possible *psychological and physical harm can be avoided*. For, unfortunately, experience has shown that these machines can be used to an extent that is excessive and unhealthy, and the content can take hold of users in a way that is morally dubious and have a negative influence. In such cases we can talk of *Excessive Use of Electronic Devices*, which I have abbreviated to EUED.

The reason why people succumb to EUED lies in the extraordinary fascination of the often fantastic opportunities offered by modern computer and information technology. The world around almost ceases to exist. All our senses, all our emotions, all our will, all our imagination, all our longings are monopolised by what is happening on the screen and the sound accompanying it. Hunger and thirst are forgotten, not to mention obligations outside the world in which we are engaged body and soul.

But what is it that creates this fascination? The way I see it is:

- The world that modern technology conjures up on our screens, in our headphones or VR helmets *presents the illusion of life*, passes itself off as life. We see other worlds, other people, fantastic beings, we can hear them and talk to them, even though they are not there in reality. What we see flashing across the screen is not real life. The appearance of some being is not a birth and its disappearance not a death; getting bigger is not growth and distortion no illness. The vibrations of the loudspeaker membrane are not human speech and the amazing ability to solve problems not thought. The artificial beings are not self-aware, living, feeling organisms. But the illusion fascinates us.

- The possibilities offered by electronic technology appear to liberate us from the basic categories of existence: *time and space*. These become relative, almost meaningless. We can practically be anywhere in the world at the same time, virtual participants in everything. In general terms the new technology makes a huge increase in the pace of life possible, in that it encourages a tendency, which is obviously deeply rooted in human nature, towards rapid changes of situation, towards intoxication with speed.

- The artificial world made possible by electronics allows the individual to extend his sphere of control enormously. He has almost everything at his fingertips— every piece of music, every piece of information, every picture, every film. Anything that promises pleasure can be consumed immediately and at little effort. Also one can solve problems, which in the past were practically insoluble, almost en passant with a few keystrokes. We can have hordes of people at our disposal as well: we press a key and the other person will talk to us as a matter of course, wherever he is and whatever he's doing. And, thanks to the virtuoso programming techniques of the specialists, with very little effort we can create all sorts of creatures, situations, actions or whole worlds and give them the features or modes of behaviour which suit us. We are able, in a way, to play at being God, being the Creator.

- Another fascinating aspect is the *combat strategy* on which most computer games are based, either against oneself, as in solitaire, against another mind, as in chess, or against an evil enemy in war games. Seen from that perspective, it is not mere chance that male computer users more often become addicted than girls and women.

- Finally, the very fact that technology can produce such *marvels* is fascinating in itself. We are gripped by the stories used, the tasks set and by the feeling of success when we have solved a problem, but we are also engrossed by the things the programmers think up, the perfection with which they have been executed and also, it appears, by the intoxicating background noise.

The extent to which EUED is *harmful* cannot be determined objectively, since any harm that occurs only affects specific individuals and they might learn from experience. What is necessary is to point out *dangers*, and in that respect we must distinguish between dangers inherent in EUED itself and dangers inherent in using particular content. First of all, the fundamental dangers, without regard to specific content:

- In general, when using electronic devices we remain aware in one way or another that we are living in an artificial world. But anyone who is addicted to EUED will become increasingly caught up in an *unreal world* and be in danger of gradually *losing the ability to distinguish between reality and illusion*. The Japanese boy who wanted to play at being Superman and jumped out of a high-rise building illustrates the extreme. A realistic view of oneself is replaced by fantasies of omnipotence. Anyone who lives in an unreal world will gradually lose their essential contact with the real world and will develop little inclination to accept responsibility in it.

- Anyone who spends hours, or even days sitting at a computer screen must expect eventual *eye and posture problems.* In addition there is optical and acoustic *over-stimulation,* caused by crazy flickering and infernal noise, which can cause general nervousness, insomnia or other health problems. Overtiredness can impair concentration and excessive time spent on the computer can lead to neglect of normal obligations. Not least this can affect behaviour in class and school work.

- It is only a short step from EUED to actual *addiction.* Addiction to computers, the Internet, games, shares the familiar problems of other addictions: complete dependence, loss of contact with reality, physical harm.

- EUED *prevents* children from occupying themselves with activities which are important for their healthy psychological development, simply through lack of time and energy. It is practical things that become neglected, for example reading books, conversations and communal activities with family and friends, practising a musical instrument, going for walks, occupying themselves with plants and animals.

- By their very nature young people tend to be susceptible to mass phenomena and manipulation by fashionable trends. Modern mass communications encourage a trend towards uniform thought and influence children and adolescents subliminally into a particular way of thinking and behaving. These trends run counter to the educational goal of enabling pupils to think for themselves and act on their own initiative.

In addition there are the dangers which come from specific games, images and manipulative Internet sites. It is not surprising that these modern lifestyle aids bear the stamp of mankind — they have everything from the highest to the lowest. They can foster a sense of community and they can serve gangs of crooks. Via the Internet one can find out and talk about basic questions of philosophy and theology, about art and literature; one can also sink into the deepest mire of depravity and criminality. There are all kinds of 'scenes' and the danger for our children is that they will be drawn into one of the pernicious scenes and get stuck there. For example: pornography of all kinds, violence, drugs, rebellion against all authority, fraud, political extremism, racism, encouragement to commit suicide.

Anyone who plays down the problem by objecting that these things have always existed, is missing an important difference. In the past, participation in one of these 'scenes', even establishing a connection with it, took a great effort just finding information. For my generation, for example, drugs were not an issue because we knew nothing about the drug scene of the time and would have found it almost impossible to gain access to it anyway. It is their easy availability that has made drugs a problem. The Internet has made information about everything, not just about useful things, *extremely accessible*. Minimal movements of the right index finger are enough to take one to the relevant web pages and from there one can be guided right round the 'scene'. And all this can happen without the parents noticing anything at all. Normal curiosity can be the start of a fatal slide into a pernicious 'scene'.

As an example we can take the 'Pro Ana' webpages. On them anorexic young girls encourage each other in their determination to avoid eating until they are nothing but skin and bone. Some have their own websites which are cleverly seductive. The illness, *anorexia nervosa*, is personified and appears as Ana, a helpful friend: 'Hi, let me introduce myself. My name's Anorexia Nervosa, but you can call me Ana. I hope we're going to be good friends.' The girls are told how to conceal Ana from their parents. There are competitions to see who can lose the most weight. For these girls, being Ana means belonging to a sworn community which keeps itself secret from the world outside and has only *one* goal: to eat nothing at all, or as little as possible. 'Don't you dare even go close to food!' it says in large letters on one of these websites and, on another, 'You can never be too thin.' And any girl who 'weakens' or, even worse, tells her parents, is branded a renegade, a traitor. Not surprisingly the clinics that specialise in this illness are full to bursting and dealing with younger and younger girls and more and more difficult cases. And the cost of healthcare is going up and up.

As this example suggests, the time is ripe for a wider discussion of a topic that has been practically excluded from educational discourse: *seduction*. In my opinion the Internet and certain computer games represent an immense machinery of seduction, far beyond anything there has ever been before. And the seductive force is so great that well-meaning parents, who want to bring up their children to the best of their ability, are powerless against it.

And that brings us to the question of how schools should deal with these phenomena and problems.

It is the same as with all social problems: we need a twofold strategy. On the one hand we must employ any countermeasures available, on the other we must seek out the causes of the problem and try to deal with them. In public discussions these two strategies tend to be regarded as mutually exclusive. I see this as mistaken, not because I think one of the standpoints is wrong, but because of the way both sides make a point of rejecting their 'opponent's' position as ineffective. But organisms, and likewise any social structure, can only survive if — however difficult it is — they satisfy *both* requirements: to remove harmful causes by developing positive strategies and to ward off negative influences.

Let us begin with the second. What countermeasures should we take? Immediately I hear the standard cry of: 'Bans are ineffective!' I see that in less absolute terms: bans alone are not effective enough. But they do have a certain effectiveness — provided in the first place that we are convinced we have the right to ban something and in the second that we have the determination to carry the ban through. The legislators clearly share this point of view and have banned the glorification of violence and child pornography. And the state quite rightly punishes those who flout these laws.

Now it is in the nature of the Internet that bans can hardly be implemented against the *producers* of criminal material. Provided they have the knowledge, anyone can distribute their material over the World Wide Web from almost anywhere on earth, they do not need an ISP. And they can do it in states where the authorities themselves are corrupt or which lack the means to take effective measures against them. Thus well-regulated states with their laws based on human rights are sidestepped and any crook has access to any child's bedroom, however remote. Despite that, every state should take all the steps that lie within its power.

Since the amount of seductive material available can only be prevented to a limited extent, all that is left — unfortunately — is to make its improper use a punishable offence. Various states have done this in the case of child pornography.

Schools also have some scope for regulation. It is my view that there should be restrictions on the use of mobile telephones and other electronic devices within the whole school area, even a complete ban if need be. That is what happens today in many workplaces, on the principle of: 'You were taken on to be *present* with your *attention* and your *labour*.' And something similar is true of schools: 'You come to school to be *present* and to concentrate on what is required of you.' It is true that there will always be recalcitrant pupils who have never learnt to regard a ban as binding on everyone and can send text messages with their hands in their pockets. But they won't be able to use the little screen to show off their latest pictures.

In January 2007 both the combined pupils' organisations in Switzerland and the umbrella organisation of Swiss teachers spoke out in the press against the ban on mobile telephones that had been introduced in certain schools. Both used the same argument, namely that young people ought to learn at school how to use mobile phones sensibly. We have here a prime example of the way the two standpoints — getting to the causes and setting limits — are seen as mutually exclusive.

That the pupils are against the regulation is not surprising, but it is astonishing for the teachers to take the same line. It is certainly correct to say that pupils should 'learn to use mobile telephones sensibly', it sounds good and puts anyone who says that in a superior moral position. But one does wonder whether those who use that argument are not deceiving themselves. Equipping pupils with knowledge and technical skills is one thing, but trying to influence their moral behaviour is entirely different. In the first case success is largely in our own hands, in the second, however, the outcome of our efforts is uncertain because an individual's morality is a matter of his own free decision. However convincingly we describe what it means to use a mobile sensibly, the pupils' behaviour is to a large extent outside our influence. That means that, despite the teachers' determination to teach them the sensible use of a mobile telephone, many will not act on it.

If this did not have serious repercussions for our work in the classroom, we could let the matter rest, rather in the same way as we do as a matter of course with questions such as healthy eating, handling tobacco and alcohol, conservation, sexuality. On those topics, too, we try to teach our pupils what is sensible, but how far they will behave sensibly is outside our influence.

But unreasonable use of mobile telephones does hamper our work in the classroom. Even if we manage (by a ban, of course) to stop phones signalling a call during lessons, the conversations, text messages, pictures and videos the technology can receive will capture the pupils' emotional life to such an extent that it will be difficult to get them to concentrate on their work. Also the openness to new things discussed in Chapter 11 will be a complete illusion. One only has to imagine everything that can be done with mobiles during the twenty minutes of break and how it will still be buzzing around in the class in the next lesson to wonder how, in such conditions, productive educational work can take place.

I also believe that the restriction of the use of mobile telephones within the school area that I am recommending here would contribute to the very desirable goal of helping the pupils to handle this advanced technological device properly.

I consider that a similar regulation to this in respect of the school's computers is also advisable. They should be set up, supervised and checked in such a way that misuse is at least very difficult.

Of course, these measures alone will not solve the problem. The most we can do is to prevent the worst effects. In fact I do not believe that the problems I have addressed here can be solved as a whole. It is the way things are: we have always had to reap what we sow. All we can expect are partial successes which will help at least some young people to find a better way in life.

That leaves us with the principal question teachers must ask themselves: *What positive, constructive measures can protect children from EUED and its negative consequences?*

The first advice we are always given is: *information*. Behind that is the old illusion that rational insight is the main motive for acting sensibly. If someone knows something is harmful, they will avoid it. If only things were like that! Unfortunately information often produces the opposite result, for it make susceptible pupils aware of the phenomenon and all its possibilities and — out of curiosity, perhaps urged on by an inclination to do the opposite of what they are told — they will experiment and, if it comes to the worst, get stuck with it. It is naive to think that a complex problem like EUED can be solved by passing on the relevant information.

The motives for acting in a way that is morally good lie in our inner being. Therefore one can only tackle the problem adequately if the development of the pupils' inner being is accepted and realised as a fundamental goal of teaching throughout the school. Every specific problem — dealing with other people, with sexuality, with fashion, the media, drugs, the Internet, mobile phones — can only be tackled successfully through education if the positive foundations have been sufficiently developed. And these foundations consist of the all-round, harmonious development of head, heart and hand which, following Pestalozzi, has been the theme of this book.

If, in this process, we do not simply *provide* information for the pupils, but *discuss* it with them, we will be moving in the right direction. Discussion does not proceed solely on the objective level, but allows all those concerned to express themselves subjectively. What we are dealing with here are embarrassment, fears, hopes, expectations, help, experiences, encounters. Good discussion creates an atmosphere of acceptance and stimulates the good side of all involved. If there is a real teacher in the classroom, and not just a subject-transmission machine, then frequent discussion will be at the heart of his teaching. And this kind of discussion is the vessel in which all the problems affecting the pupils can be considered in a spirit of mutual acceptance, even friendship. Thus we can talk openly and honestly about seduction, which exists in other areas apart from EUED, and demonstrate the sensible use of electronic devices. In this the teacher has the right — and the duty even — to become involved as a person: with the whole weight of his experience of life and his authority resting on his trustworthiness. For true education, which can change and develop people from inside, is always founded on personal relationships. For these reasons discussion,

understood in the right spirit, is the only way open to schools of protecting their pupils from EUED or persuading them to give it up. There is
no guarantee it will be successful.

This brings us back once more to the point of the problematic
nature of the system of using specialist subject teachers, which becomes
increasingly general at precisely the age at which EUED can become
acute. In which subject should the process I describe above be carried
out? In the classes on the mother tongue, of course, or in those other subjects that deal with the real world, citizenship or whatever the subjects
are called. But there is no question that a teacher who takes the whole
range, or most, of the subjects with a class is in a better position. Finally,
we must face up to the fact that schools have a double role to fulfil: to
transmit knowledge and skills, and to contribute to children's upbringing. As far as the transmission of knowledge and skills is concerned, the
system of subject teachers has the advantage that a specialist is taking the class; but as far as contributing to the children's upbringing is
concerned, the class teacher is in the better position, since he has much
greater opportunity of forming a personal relationship with each pupil.
Bearing the current pressing social problems in mind, those in charge
of educational policy would be well advised to review their preferences.

'Counting and doing sums is the basis of all order inside our heads.'

25 **Where's My Calculator?**

The glass cost 28 francs, the shop assistant said, but there was a discount of 25% on a dozen. 'That makes 21 francs a glass,' I said. The young lady looked at me in astonishment and said, 'Yes, it'll be something like that.' Then she went over to the counter, picked up the calculator, typed in 28, divided by 100, multiplied by 25 and said, almost in amazement. 'The discount is seven francs, yes, you're right, that makes 21 francs.'

Traditional arithmetic is dead and buried and has been replaced by mathematics. That means that when experienced instructors wring their hands and complain that their apprentices are hardly able to do sums, we can proudly reply, 'True, they can't do sums, but they can think.'

It has always made me furious when people suggest that the ability to do sums has nothing to do with thinking. I remember an eleven-year-old who had a very poor memory and once more couldn't remember what 7 x 8 was. His solution was as follows: 'I'll try doing 8 x 8, that's the same as 4 x 16 and that's 2 x 32, equals 64. Take away 8, that makes 56.' And if that's not thinking, I'm a Dutchman.

In the late 1960s arithmetic was subjected to a fundamental critical review and the syllabus and course books throughout Switzerland were revised in accordance with the latest trends. It is often suggested that what sparked off this total review of traditional arithmetic teaching was the 'Sputnik shock' the Americans suffered in 1957 when they realised the Russians were clearly superior to them in science and technology.

At the time there were three main arguments against the traditional teaching concentrating on arithmetic:

Firstly, it was complained that arithmetic *fixed the pupils' thought processes* in very specific channels and hampered the development of true mathematical thinking. Mathematical thinking was *flexible, general and creative*, it was said, and could not be developed by concentrating on the number system and familiarising pupils with it by means of the basic operations. The important thing was to teach pupils how to deal with abstract quantities and logical relationships. Thus set theory — until then an area of higher mathematics that was taught at university – was declared the foundation of mathematics as a whole and of maths teaching. An American, Professor Dienes, designed 'logic blocks' as a basis for practical exercises.

The *second* complaint was that the teaching fixed arithmetic on the *decimal system*, which, it was said, was only *one* possibility among many — and — from a mathematical point of view — quite arbitrarily chosen. The use of the binary system in computer technology showed that it was necessary to loosen the hold of the decimal system over arithmetic.

Thirdly, it was at about the same time that the first electronic pocket calculators appeared on the market. That made it look as if modern people no longer needed to be able to do sums, since the machine could do everything more quickly and more reliably. The task of mathematics, it was claimed, was to teach pupils to understand arithmetical processes, but the actual calculations could happily be left to the machine.

These arguments were accepted in Switzerland, even though there was no comparison between the quality of teaching here and that in American public schools. Apart from that, I question all three arguments from a psychological and an educational point of view.

Firstly, our minds need thought routines if they are to be creative at all. We have to learn how to make logical deductions. If pupils vary this by doing thousands of sums, we are not fixing their thought processes, we are giving them the equipment to make future, more complex thought processes more manageable, even to make them possible. In mathematics the fundamental thought routines consist in dealing with number concepts and the basic operations. Naturally those elementary relationships between sets which can be demonstrated using the logic blocks are part of this. But it is certainly wrong to maintain that this abstract approach will enable a child to solve more concrete arithmetical problems.

Secondly, from the point of view of psychology, the decimal system is not an arbitrary product but is derived from our ten fingers. Relating it to this physical reality is, from a psychological and educational point of view, elementary in the truest sense of the word. An abstract concept is anchored in our own body and any other system depends on the basic idea and the linguistic conventions of the decimal system for us to be able to understand it. Children need an inner yardstick to help them find their way into another numerical system. In addition to that, in any area of learning children need to establish fixed points from which they can extend their knowledge and skills. This is especially important for less gifted children. Otherwise all we will do is produce failures.

Thirdly, the calculator cannot replace 'mental arithmetic', for without a clear conception of numbers we will be unable to interpret the mechanically produced series of figures adequately as numbers and values. Beyond that, there are many calculations we need to do in the course of our everyday lives for which we cannot constantly be taking out our pocket calculator. And finally, mental arithmetic serves the more general purpose — in Pestalozzi's system — of helping to develop our faculties: our imagination, our ability to store abstract material for short periods, our ability to deal in our minds with abstractions, our ability to concentrate. Education is not about producing results as quickly as possible, it is about our thought processes as such, for it is only by thinking that we can develop our ability to think.

During the last couple of decades the influence of the ideological positions that dominated the sixties and seventies has gradually receded. What it has left behind, in my opinion, are three relics which are partly responsible for our school leavers' unsatisfactory arithmetical skills:

No longer requiring the individual steps to be expressed in language. When a pupil is given the problem of calculating the price of 7 kilos of goods, for which he has been given the price for 5 kilos, he needs to recognise the proportion 7:5 and to apply that to the price. If

199

you insist, it can be expressed as a formula, but no one can get round the fact that you have to divide the price of the goods by 5 and multiply the result by 7. Leaving aside simple addition and subtraction, this is the basic model for most mathematical problems faced by people today in their private life and in their work. It is in the true sense of the word an *elementary* calculation. Despite that, experience shows that many people find it almost impossible to solve such problems, or at least can only do so with great difficulty, especially when the actual figures are a little more complex.

It would help if educational theory did not reject a method simply because it had been used for decades, even centuries. Until the above-mentioned revolution in the teaching of mathematics in the 1970s, in Switzerland, the land of Pestalozzi, it was customary — and especially helpful for mathematically less gifted children — for pupils to be trained to express the individual steps of this type of calculation in language:

* 5 kilograms of potatoes cost 9 francs
* 1 kilogram of potatoes costs 9 francs ÷ 5 = 1.80 francs
* 7 kilograms of potatoes cost 7 x 1.80 francs = 12.60 francs

The almost complete elimination of the linguistic expression of calculations does a disservice to children. Everything that is done in mathematics at this level should be expressible in language. Then pupils' thinking will be founded on clear conceptions. The three brief sentences in the example given represent the stages of a correct logical deduction.

The abolition of the distinction between measuring and partitioning in division. That is all very well for a mathematician, who thinks in purely abstract terms and does not visualise anything specific under the factors or the operator 'times', but for pupils, who first of all have to understand how it all works, not distinguishing between the two aspects is fatal. Every calculation and every operator must be based on an *action* that is comprehensible in physical terms and can be visualised. Whatever the 'new mathematicians' may say, cutting a length of three metres up into sixty equal parts, for example, is not the same as ascertaining how many units of sixty centimetres are contained in the three metres. This obvious fact needs an equivalent in the mathematical representation, including the linguistic formulation: in the first case we are partitioning, in the second measuring. That is, the division operator has two meanings which must be clearly distinguished logically and linguistically.

Similarly, the multiplication operator must have a meaning which can be carried out as action and as visualisation. This is only possible when the first factor is the multiplier: if there are seven rulers, each of thirty centimetres, on the table, then the multiplicand (which is always the second factor) is repeated seven times. Whatever the commutative law might say, for beginners, who need to be able to base their thinking on actions and visualisations, the sum 'thirty times seven centimetres' is simply wrong, even though it produces the right result.

Pupils must also learn to see that when they are dividing they are inverting an actual or conceivable multiplication. Then they can say: If I make the *first* factor (the multiplier) the divisor, I am *partitioning* and the result is the multiplicand. If, on the other hand, I make the *second* factor (the multiplicand) the divisor, I am *measuring* and the result is the multiplier. Not distinguishing between measuring and partitioning has *not* led to more mathematical thinking, but to unclear dealing with numbers that is not founded on visualisation. It is the children who suffer, above all the weaker ones, who particularly need to start out from concrete actions and visualisation.

The general devaluation of arithmetic, of working things out in one's head and learning tables off by heart. This is a result of the extension of the range and variety of mathematical subject matter and exercises. There is no doubt that this makes mathematics lessons more varied and interesting — especially for the more gifted pupils. Unfortunately it simply leaves too little time to practise the elementary skills. We are therefore tempted to ask, would less not perhaps be more?

At the foundation stages of arithmetic I have had excellent results with the Cuisenaire method. This proceeds *analytically* rather than *synthetically*. The starting point is never a precise question, such as 'What does six times seven make?' but a result: 'What are all the things that make forty-two?' Central to it is the observation of numbers. The synthetic procedure only allows *one* solution to a problem, while with the analytical method the problem is left *completely open*. That means there are hardly any limits set on the pupils' freedom and creativity and that particularly increases their motivation. It also means that pupils of different ability can work at their own level, without the threat of failure.

I would prefer not to have to tell a critic of our school system what I quoted at the beginning of this chapter: 'True, they can't do sums, but they can think.' I would like to be able to say, 'Since they have learnt to think, they can also do sums.'

'The God of my mind is a mere construct of the mind; I know no God but the God of my heart.'

26 The 'Gretchen Question'

The source of the 'Gretchen question' — a question or discussion about someone's religious convictions — can be found in Goethe's play. Gretchen asks Faust, 'And what about your religion?' Faust's answer is evasive and we are tempted to use the same tactic. Religion in school? In a state school? Is there any question of that nowadays?

Fifty years ago there was no question about it. Prayers were said at the beginning and end of school, in Catholic areas there was a cross on the wall and religious instruction was — along with that for the various confessions — part of the official syllabus. And if anyone offended against Christian morality, it was quite natural for a teacher to quote the Ten Commandments.

Naturally there are schools where that is still the case, but in general, conditions are markedly different, for in the meantime a fundamental social change has taken place. The ties that the population previously had as a matter of course with one church or another have weakened significantly. Traditional Christian ideas of sin and its consequences are no longer the basis of the moral attitudes of the majority. Most religious observances within the family and in public have been discontinued. For the public in general the distinctions between the various churches have blurred and the barriers between the churches have fallen correspondingly. The authority of ecclesiastical institutions has sunk to a minimum. A large proportion of those who describe themselves as religious have distanced themselves from traditional tenets and include elements of other churches, religions

205

or philosophies in their beliefs. Foreign religions have taken up residence in the formerly Christian West. Publicly acknowledged lack of religious belief is socially acceptable. Religion is considered a private matter and only appears peripherally in public discussion of politics, science or the arts.

In this environment it is hardly possible to reach a consensus on any function religion might have in state education. What first comes to mind is tolerance: anyone who wants to have a religion should practice it in private, anywhere they like, apart from in school. Schools should be a religion-free zone.

But if we think that, we are deceiving ourselves. There are religious cultures for which tolerance is not a desirable quality. They insist on being allowed to live out their religious convictions in school as well. Teachers are directly confronted with this: girls want to wear religious symbols and not take part in gymnastics or swimming lessons or school camps; pupils in primary one refuse to write a 't' because it is a cross; parents protest when candles are lit at Christmas, carols sung and Christmas stories read, while others demand that in science the Biblical story of the creation should replace evolution or at least be taught as an alternative theory.

These developments leave schools in a no-win situation. The clash between intolerance and tolerance will lead either to conflict or to the victory of intolerance and the loser will be our teaching, for education in the tradition of enlightened humanism is not possible either in an atmosphere of intolerance or on the basis of a struggle for power. Teachers must not be left to deal with this situation alone, it is politicians who must meet the challenge.

It was easier for Pestalozzi. He could at least assume a consensus of the majority of the population regarding Christianity or at least religion in general. For him there was no doubt about it: the education of the whole person, as he understood it, is fundamentally religious. *'I am convinced my aims will only flourish in religious soil'* he wrote in 1808 to Ignaz Heinrich von Wessenberg, the vicar-general of the diocese of Constance. And in his main work on educational method, *Wie Gertrud ihre Kinder lehrt* (How Gertrude Teaches her Children, 1800) he calls the question of the relationship between his method of education and the development of reverence for God *'the keystone of my whole system'*. Correspondingly, he regards the most profound goal of the education of the heart as 'faith and love' and combines the two goals of moral education and reverence for God in the concept of 'moral-religious education'. For him, then, 'the faculties of the heart' are not, as is often assumed nowadays, the emotions as such, but our 'moral-religious powers'.

We must remember that Pestalozzi did not see 'God' primarily as a power ruling the world from above, but as an inner light at work within the human heart. He regarded God as *'the closest relationship of mankind'*, that is, not as a supernatural being, but as a reality we can feel in our own hearts. His 'moral-religious education' was designed to enable young people, as they grew up, to hear and love *'God in their innermost being'*. He saw this form of the love of God as the surest basis for ethical behaviour. Thus he wrote in 1782, in a little essay on religion in his own periodical *Ein Schweizer Blatt*: *If you forget God, you forget yourself, for the love of God is your life, O mortal — it is the bond that ties the powers of your heart and your head, and if this sacred bond of your powers should break, it will mean they will fall apart and that will be the source of the sin that will kill you, O man! Therefore guard well the source of your life and the bond of your noblest powers and love God. Look around you, O mortal, and see what is the man who does not love God.*

And then he goes on to describe the consequences of godlessness: unhappiness, despair, self-destruction. *'The bonds of life are bonds of virtue and they tear apart when a man does not honour God.'*

Anyone who aims at 'education in the spirit of Pestalozzi' cannot afford to ignore these remarks that are central to his outlook. They must at least ask themselves: could it be the case that Pestalozzi's judgment is correct? Could it be that those people who were educated in that spiritual ethos and are willing to justify their lives before God might indeed in general behave in a more socially responsible manner than those who reject the idea of a divine inner voice without even considering it; could it be that they are more likely to reject violence, to show more respect for their fellow human beings, to be more persistent in the pursuit of peace, more ready to accept responsibility or to show a caring attitude to the world around?

Should Pestalozzi be right, would it not be sensible, given the urgent social and moral problems of the present, to consider whether, and in what new forms, religious concepts could be included in the education system.

Against the background of the social change mentioned above and the legal situation of state schools, it is no longer possible to insist on the tenets of specific churches, or even specifically Christian ones. What is needed is what is common to all religions: the awareness of the existence of an all-embracing power and the willingness to justify our lives before it as the ultimate inner authority — which expresses itself in our conscience.

Only teachers who have a positive emotional relationship with their pupils can talk credibly about *conscience* and listening to one's own inner voice. Such a relationship is characterised by mutual respect or affection. On that basis it is possible to examine the question of what grounds there are for a person to do good and eschew evil. I have come across pupils who saw only one single reason not to steal the goods in the supermarket: they didn't want to be caught. I have also come across pupils of sixteen who, as far as they were aware, were hearing the word 'conscience' for the first time — and had no idea what it meant.

Conscience can only be developed in a *culture of quiet*. If, as a teacher, one cannot manage to get one's class to feel the beneficial effects of true quiet, talking about conscience will just degenerate into preaching morality. It will not reach the pupils' centre. Fortunate are the pupils who, together with their teacher, can be quiet, listen to what is inside themselves and express what they have heard without having to hold back. This intimacy is, in a way, the antithesis of the increasing hustle and bustle and depersonalisation in modern education.

At the centre of a culture of quiet is *meditation*. It is a place where religious and non-religious people can meet. It is free from any kind of dogmatism or ideology. Teaching that is founded on the spirit of Pestalozzi always offers opportunities for moments of meditative contemplation.

This culture of quiet and the habit of meditative moments is also in contrast to the increasingly brutal nature of society which expresses itself on the one hand in its simplistic language with trite superlatives and on the other in its coarse way of addressing others and, ultimately, in psychological and physical violence. I really do not know of any other way of setting young men, who can do nothing but use their fists, on the road to showing understanding and consideration for others, than by gently introducing them to the possibility of quietening down, of listening to what is inside themselves.

Religion does have a legitimate place in school in a more limited way, namely as part of our cultural heritage. To be interested in religion and its expressions, one does not have to be any more religious than one has to be a Marxist to study Marxism. Anyone who refuses to concern themselves with religion at all is ignoring a central element of human life and therefore lacks a key to the understanding of important historical circumstances, of notable social phenomena and of major works of literature, art and music. Whether one regards the Bible as a divine revelation or not, knowledge of the Bible facilitates the understanding of countless cultural phenomena. Seen in this perspective, it is as reasonable to expect a Muslim to familiarise himself with the Bible as a Christian to read the Koran.

Similarly, it is part of a person's education not only to learn the biographies of people who were guided by ideologies, but also the lives of people who drew strength from their relation with God. I do not see why our pupils should learn something about Hitler, Lenin or Mao but hardly anything about Theresa of Avila, Francis of Assisi, Edith Stein, Maximilian Kolbe, Abbé Pierre or Cardinal Galen who, in the most difficult times, sought for a way that could combine Christian action, patriotism and the struggle against Nazi ideology.

Young people look for *models*, a fact well known to the modern entertainment industry, which exploits that need to the full. Every teacher who acquaints his pupils with the biographies of people who obeyed the dictates of their conscience, were true to their ethical principles or lived out their religious faith in their lives, gives young people a yardstick against which to measure things. Perhaps they will discover potentialities within themselves which will make them strive for higher things than merely shining in the limelight.

Any teacher, even a non-religious one, can make full use of the suggestions I have made here. A teacher with religious convictions must observe restraint. Propaganda for his beliefs would be just as much an abuse of power as propaganda for a political ideology. As is well known, every standpoint has its opposite, and honesty demands that we present both as objectively as possible. So far, so good. But as long as a teacher attempts to satisfy that demand, there is one right one cannot refuse him, namely the right to *bear witness*. Here, too, he must show restraint, but there will be occasions when a teacher will tell his pupils why he does one thing and not another, and a teacher with religious convictions will leave his pupils in no doubt as to where he draws his strength from and to whom he feels he owes responsibility.

'A person who needs to have patience as a teacher is a poor thing. He should have love and joy.'

27 **What Everything Depends On**

Did the jigsaw pieces build up into a picture? The picture of a school that has freed itself from the many constraints which come from the countless political measures seen as absolutely necessary? The picture of a school in which learning is a pleasure and teaching is a pleasure? A school in which human beings — teachers and pupils — can become involved in their own distinctive individuality? A school which has made Pestalozzi's 'educated humanity' its ultimate goal?

There is much that could still be said: on the marking system, on the teaching of individual subjects and on fashions in teaching theory, on learning foreign languages in a way that is appropriate for children, on the development of teachers' and pupils' creativity, on the problem of handwriting, on the importance of music in schools, on dealing with children who are non-native speakers, on working together with parents, on the authorities' relationship with teachers, on the problems of part-time teachers, on the lack of male teachers in primary schools, on education vouchers, that would allow private institutions also to cater for the less well-off.

But enough is enough. One thing is certain, however: a good school can only exist with good, motivated and also talented teachers. If those in charge of educational policy believe there is a shortage of such teachers and therefore organise education in such a way that it can operate without good teachers, they are going down the wrong road. What they ought to be asking themselves is what must be done to ensure that schools get the teachers they need. But the state will not get better teachers with a teacher-training system that is organised on mechanical lines and puts its main emphasis on acquiring knowledge. It will not get better teachers if it clings to the belief that the teaching profession is just like any other and that everything that is necessary for it can be 'delivered' in teacher training and in-service courses. And it will not get better teachers if it keeps them on an even tighter rein and marks them according to some assessment system, giving points for ticking this or that box, and even makes salary levels or special bonuses dependent on it.

I believe using such measures to try and motivate teachers to improve their work is the wrong way. A bricklayer's performance can be measured: how long and how high is the piece of wall he has done today? But a teacher's performance cannot be measured. A true teacher is like a farmer scattering his seed over a long, narrow field, marching on and never looking back. He knows, as he carries on with his task, that much of what he is sowing will only come up after years, or even decades. Anyone who wants their work as a teacher to bear fruit should not court success or want to reap the rewards.

For what is success for a teacher? To be applauded? That is easily achieved by currying favour with the right people. To be well liked? You just have to say what people want to hear. To get good results in tests and exams? That is certainly important if it's done in the right spirit. But one can neglect many things that are important in order to spend more time drilling the class in what the pupils need to know for tests and exams.

Or do we call success getting a class through the year with no serious conflicts? Perhaps the teacher was lucky, or the worst cases were given to a colleague who had stronger nerves. Or he did not face up to problems because he did not want to disturb the superficial harmony.

Who can measure the performance of a teacher who takes the time to learn a poem off by heart before dealing with it in class? Of a teacher who is not satisfied with the material in the text book and spends days reading up on a topic? Who can measure the performance of a teacher who remains silent at a staff meeting, when a pupil's catalogue of misdeeds is being discussed, because he knows that otherwise he would lose the trust of the problem pupil?

And what about the performance of the teacher who pays for a course of psychotherapy out of his own funds to help him come to terms with his difficulties with certain children? Should he shout it from the rooftops to build up the points in his account? And what about the teacher who always senses the right moment to let drop a remark about important questions or fundamental values — off the cuff, unspectacular, but full of commitment, and effective? Should he note it down and stick it under his head of department's nose? Perhaps what he said will only take effect when his pupils are already going grey.

The spread of the points systems tempts teachers to put their work in the public eye and to make a show of things that should remain hidden. The things one can show become the things that are important. It stirs up jealousy, encourages conformism and undermines the sense of community. And the insistence on teamwork that has been forced on us is no compensation for that.

I am a realist and I know that there are also poor teachers, people who do not accept the responsibility and do not carry out their obligations satisfactorily. In such cases it is the duty of their head teachers to deal with the problem of the failing teacher. But for that there is no need of a system of qualifications or bonuses, which robs all the teachers, even the creative and responsible ones, of their independence, implying that they would be motivated to perform better by such a ridiculous points system. A teacher who has a vocation knows himself what he owes the pupils and does not have to be driven by the stick and carrot.

Let us finish by listening to Pestalozzi. As was usual at his time, he only speaks of men, but I have allowed myself to adapt it to the demands of the present day:

'One thing is needed and that is good schoolmasters and mistresses. Where they are absent, all the rest of the business of education in the land is a waste of time, so much dust to blind the men and women who do not want to see what they lack. Anyone, therefore, who really wants schools that will give the people a good education must above all set their hand to providing what is sorely needed, namely that all over the country there are men and women who are willing and able to educate and guide young people with insight and love so that they gain the wisdom they need for life and the strength and order they need for their station and their situation in life.'

Lightning Source UK Ltd.
Milton Keynes UK
20 May 2010

154449UK00002B/2/P

9 781906 924997